Mama's
ITALIAN
Family Cookbook

Mama's
ITALIAN
Family Cookbook

*Family Recipes
from Mama's Kitchen*

First published in 2013
LOVE FOOD is an imprint of Parragon Books Ltd

Parragon
Chartist House,
15-17 Trim Street,
Bath, BA1 1HA, UK

www.parragon.com/lovefood

ISBN: 978-1-78186-811-9
Printed in China

Design concept by Sabine Vonderstein, Cologne, Germany, with additional design work by Siân Williams
New photography and home economy: Mike Cooper and Lincoln Jefferson
New recipes: Beverly Le Blanc
Mama text: Dominic Utton
Senior Commissioning Editor: Cheryl Warner

Mama and all characters mentioned in this book are entirely fictitious. Any similarity to any person, living or dead, is purely coincidental and unintended.

Notes for the Reader

This book uses standard kitchen measuring spoons and cups. All spoon and cup measurements are level unless otherwise indicated. Unless otherwise stated, milk is assumed to be whole, butter is assumed to be salted, eggs are large, individual vegetables are medium, and pepper is freshly ground black pepper. Unless otherwise stated, all root vegetables should be washed and peeled before using. For the best results, use a meat thermometer when cooking meat and poultry—check the latest USDA government guidelines for current advice.

Garnishes and serving suggestions are all optional and not necessarily included in the recipe ingredients or method. The times given are only an approximate guide. Preparation times differ according to the techniques used by different people and the cooking times may also vary from those given. Optional ingredients, variations, or serving suggestions have not been included in the calculations.

Picture Acknowledgments

The publisher would like to thank the following for permission to reproduce copyright material on the following pages: Cover (Mama image): Mrs. Luisa Pierotti © CARLO BAVAGNOLI/Getty Images; page 8: Tomatoes, glass, teapot on table © Anna Nemoy (Xaomena)/Getty Images; page 9 (heart image): Rose petals forming heart shape symbol © 2009 Chaulafanita/Getty Images. All other incidentals are Istockphoto images.

Contents

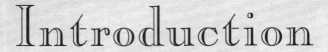

Introduction

Ciao amici! Welcome to *Mama's Italian Family Cookbook*. It's not just a collection of recipes from my own kitchen, but a scrapbook of family wisdom and a little insight into my life.

This is the second cookbook I've written, and this one is all about recreating the energy, ambience, love, and, of course, wonderful food that is only found in the heart of a true Italian family. Inside, of course, you will find many *molto delizioso* recipes, but also so much more. My cookbooks are not just about preparing meals — they're a whole way of life, a *filosofia* for *la bella vita*.

For me, there is no distinction between the cooking and the cook. The feelings, the passion, the love, and the experiences of the person making the recipes all go into the food — and so the cook becomes a part of the recipe! In other words, to understand my food is to understand me. And if there is one word that would sum me up, it's *famiglia*. Family is everything to me. That's why they call me Mama!

But I'm talking too quickly. First things first! Let me tell you about myself. I'm the head of a large, noisy, happy household here in a small village in Apulia, a province in the south of Italy. I've been married to Alberto for nearly 60 years — long before the first astronaut walked on the moon!

We live a simple life in Apulia — we don't ask for much, and we make our own happiness. And nowhere is that more true than with our *famiglia*.

Together Alberto and I have six *bambini*, 22 *nipoti*, or grandchildren, and 12 *pronipoti*, or great grandchildren. Every year brings another baby! And if that is a blessing, it is also a miracle that each of our great grandchildren are beautiful boys. Alberto often jokes that together one day our *pronipoti* will form a soccer team to rival the divine AC Milan side of 1989! I say they will be better.

Of course, I may be the head of a family of more than 40 strong (and I don't include myself or Alberto in that count, nor our many cousins, nephews, nieces, all of whom can often be found sitting at our table or harassing Mama in the kitchen!) but naturally I'm not cooking for all of them every day. Our *bambini* have families of their own now.

Still — Mama never cooks a lonely meal.
Our eldest boys, Marco and Filippo, still work the same olive groves that Alberto used to tend.

And our youngest two, Maria and Lucia, married men from the same village and live within earshot on a clear day. It is a rare day that will not see six or seven hungry mouths for me to feed!

I've lived in this village all of my life — and my Mama, her Mama, and her Mama before her all did the same. Tradition is *molto importante* here.

I love my family

And nowhere is this more clearly seen than in the kitchen. Learning how to feed a family is a skill and a passion that is passed down the generations. It is a source of pride with me that I have always put beautiful, healthy food on my table — and my family have grown strong and beautiful themselves as a result.

From simple dinners when times are hard to celebration dinners fit for presidents — coming together to eat is what Italian family life is all about. All of my experience and all of my passion are captured in the following pages — and all the experience and passion of those who taught me. And believe me when I tell you I had the best teachers in all of Italy — my Mama, and her Mama before her. It is not simply a collection of recipes, it's an expression of Italian family life.

Buon appetito!

Eccellente Antipasti & Appetizers

ntipasti means "before the meal" in Italian and is the traditional first course of any family dinner. This appetizer is the beginning of the meal, when anticipation is at its highest and, for the chef, it is the first chance you have to show what you're made of. From delicious calamari, spicy olives, or garlic bread to broths and soups, it is a time not for satisfying appetites, but instead for whetting them for the delights yet to come! Creating *eccellente* antipasti sets the tone for the whole meal. It should be like the first kiss of a passionate love affair: beautiful in itself, but only a mere taster for the joys to follow. And remember the wise words of my Mama: "la più grande opera inizia con la semplice nota" — even the grandest operas begin with the simplest notes.

Scarpariello
- - - - - - - - - - - - - - -
Chicken Wings

1. Mix together the flour and paprika in a wide dish. Season the chicken wings with salt and black pepper, then dredge them in the flour mixture, shaking off the excess.

2. Heat the oil in a large, deep skillet over medium—high heat. Add as many chicken wings as will fit in the skillet in a single layer, and sauté for 3—5 minutes, until golden brown on both sides. Remove from the skillet and set aside. Add extra oil to the skillet, if needed, and repeat until all the wings are fried.

3. Pour off all but 1 tablespoon of the oil. Add the sausages to the skillet and cook for 3—5 minutes, until brown all over. Remove from the skillet and set aside.

4. Pour off all but 1 tablespoon of the oil from the skillet. Add the onion and red bell peppers and stir for 3—5 minutes, until soft. Add the cherry peppers and garlic and stir for an additional 2 minutes, until the garlic is soft.

5. Return the chicken and sausages to the skillet. Stir in the stock, wine, lemon juice, and crushed red pepper (if using), and season with salt and pepper. Bring to a boil, cover the skillet, reduce the heat to low, and simmer for 15—20 minutes, until the wings are cooked through and the juices run clear when you cut into one with the tip of a sharp knife.

6. Using a slotted spoon, transfer the wings, sausages, red bell peppers, and cherry peppers to warm plates. Bring the liquid in the skillet to a boil, then spoon it over the meat. Garnish with parsley and serve.

SERVES 4

2 tablespoons all-purpose flour
¼ teaspoon hot paprika
24 chicken wings, trimmed
2 tablespoons olive oil, plus
   extra if needed
4 spicy Italian sausages,
   cut into 1½-inch pieces
1 onion, thinly sliced
2 red bell peppers, seeded and
   sliced
4 pickled cherry peppers,
   sliced
4 garlic cloves, sliced
½ cup chicken stock
½ cup dry white wine
2 tablespoons lemon juice
pinch of crushed red pepper
   (optional)
salt and pepper, to taste
¼ cup chopped fresh flat-leaf
   parsley, to garnish

Calamari Fritti
Fried Calamari

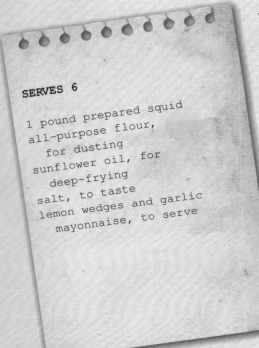

SERVES 6

1 pound prepared squid
all-purpose flour,
  for dusting
sunflower oil, for
  deep-frying
salt, to taste
lemon wedges and garlic
  mayonnaise, to serve

1. Slice the squid into ½-inch rings and halve the tentacles if large. Rinse under cold running water and pat dry with paper towels. Dust the squid rings with flour so that they are lightly coated.

2. Heat the oil in a deep-fat fryer or heavy saucepan to 350—375°F, or until a cube of bread browns in 30 seconds. Fry the squid rings, in batches, turning several times, for 2—3 minutes, or until golden brown and crisp all over. Do not overcook because the squid will become tough and rubbery instead of moist and tender.

3. Remove with a slotted spoon and drain well on paper towels. Keep warm while you fry the remaining squid rings.

4. Sprinkle the fried squid rings with salt and serve piping hot, accompanied by lemon wedges for squeezing over the rings and garlic mayonnaise for dipping.

Mama's Tip:
If you like your calamari to have some more zing, add a pinch of cayenne pepper to the flour.

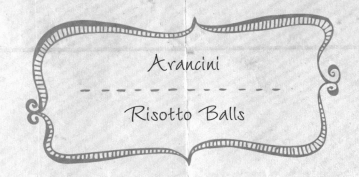

Arancini

- - - - - - - - - -

Risotto Balls

1. Heat the oil with 2 tablespoons of the butter in a deep saucepan. Add the onion and cook, stirring frequently, for 5 minutes, or until softened.

2. Add the rice and mix to coat in oil and butter. Cook, stirring continuously, for 2—3 minutes, or until the grains are translucent.

3. Gradually add the hot stock, a ladleful at a time. Add more liquid as the rice absorbs each addition. Cook, stirring, for 20 minutes, or until all the liquid is absorbed and the rice is creamy.

4. Remove from the heat and add the remaining butter. Mix well, then stir in the Parmesan until it melts. Season with salt and pepper. Let cool completely.

5. Place 1 tablespoon of the risotto in the palm of your hand. Top with a cube of mozzarella, then place another tablespoon of risotto on top. Press together to form a ball, making sure that the filling is completely enclosed. Repeat until all the risotto and mozzarella have been used.

6. Chill the risotto balls for 10 minutes, then dip in the egg. Drain and coat in the bread crumbs, shaking off any excess. Chill for 10 minutes.

7. Heat enough oil for deep-frying in a large saucepan or deep-fat fryer to 350—375°F, or until a cube of bread browns in 30 seconds. Carefully drop in the risotto balls, in batches, and cook for 5 minutes, until golden brown.

8. Remove the risotto balls from the oil with a slotted spoon, then drain on paper towels. Let cool slightly before serving.

SERVES 4

1 tablespoon olive oil
3 tablespoons butter
1 small onion, finely chopped
2⅓ cups risotto rice
8¾ cups vegetable stock
⅔ cup freshly grated
   Parmesan cheese
1 cup cubed mozzarella cheese
1 egg, beaten
2 cups fresh bread crumbs
oil, for deep-frying
salt and pepper, to taste

Mama's guide to the perfect family party

They say the perfect party needs three things: the best people, the best food, and the best hostess. Well, when the guests are famiglia and the hostess is Mama, you're more than halfway there! And, of course, with Mama's recipes, the food is certain to be the best, too.

So how does Mama host the perfect family party? Follow my easy pointers and you won't go wrong.

First, remember that parties are supposed to be fun! Even if organizing a big get-together can feel a little stressante, always keep in mind why you're doing it. These are your nearest and dearest, your most beloved. Everything will be fine.

Families, of course, expand— and although in Apulia everyone knows each other's business, there may still be girlfriends, boyfriends, partners, or friends who don't know everyone present. Mama has a trick when introducing two strangers. Say their names and then think of something they have in common: "Beppe, this is Alfredo. Alfredo's cousin works with you in Napoli, I believe ..."

It's not just about you. Sure, you're the hostess, but everyone's here to have a good time. Let the party flow to its own rhythm; you don't have to be everywhere at once!

Hostessing a party does not mean spending all your time in the kitchen. You should enjoy yourself, too! Once all the main jobs are done, relax and have a glass of Chianti.

Evviva!

RERS

19

Although things should develop at their own pace, be strict with the food. If it is a stand-up party, keep the nibbles well stocked and be sure all your guests sample some. If you are sitting to eat, call everyone to the table promptly.

Finally and più importante, don't forget to keep the vino flowing for everyone else! This is Alberto's department—but Mama likes to make sure he's keeping everyone's glass topped up!

Bruschetta con Funghi
Mushroom Bruschetta

SERVES 4

4 slices sourdough bread, such as Pugliese
3 garlic cloves, 1 halved and 2 minced
3 tablespoons extra virgin olive oil
8 ounces mixed wild mushrooms, such as porcini and portobello
2 tablespoons butter
1 small onion, finely chopped
¼ cup dry white wine
salt and pepper, to taste
2 tablespoons chopped fresh flat-leaf parsley, to garnish

1. Preheat the broiler to medium. Toast the bread slices under the preheated broiler on both sides.

2. Rub the bread with the garlic halves and drizzle with 2 tablespoons of the oil. Keep warm.

3. Wipe the mushrooms thoroughly to remove any trace of soil and slice any large ones.

4. Heat the remaining oil with half of the butter in a skillet. Add the mushrooms and cook over medium heat, stirring, for 3—4 minutes, until soft. Remove with a slotted spoon and keep warm.

5. Heat the remaining butter in the skillet. Add the onion and chopped garlic and cook, stirring, for 3—4 minutes, until soft. Add the wine, stir, and let simmer for 2—3 minutes, until reduced.

6. Return the mushrooms to the skillet and heat through. The sauce should be thick enough to glaze the mushrooms. Season with salt and pepper.

7. Pile the mushrooms on top of the toasted bread, sprinkle with the parsley, and serve immediately.

1. Preheat the oven to 350°F.

2. Mix together the butter, garlic, and parsley in a bowl until well combined. Season with pepper and mix well.

3. Make several cuts lengthwise in the bread, but be careful not to cut all the way through.

4. Spread the flavored butter over one side of each cut and place the loaf on a large sheet of aluminum foil on a baking sheet.

5. Wrap up the bread in the foil and bake in the preheated oven for 10—15 minutes, or until the butter melts and the bread is piping hot. Let cool on a wire rack for 5 minutes, then serve immediately.

SERVES 6

1¼ sticks butter, softened
3 garlic cloves, crushed
2 tablespoons chopped fresh flat-leaf parsley
pepper, to taste
1 large or 2 small sticks of Italian bread

Mama's Tip:
If the bread will be eaten with a tomato-based dish, replace half of the parsley with chopped fresh basil.

Bruschetta e Olive Piccante
Spicy Olives with Bruschetta

SERVES 4

4½ cups finely chopped, pitted
ripe black olives

2 sun-dried tomatoes in olive oil,
drained and thinly sliced

1-2 red chiles, seeded and
finely chopped

grated rind of 2 lemons

extra virgin olive oil,
for soaking and brushing

4 large slices sourdough bread
or country-style bread, halved

2 garlic cloves, halved

4 scallions, finely chopped

sea salt and pepper, to taste

1. Combine the olives, tomatoes, chiles, and lemon rind in a nonmetallic bowl. Season with pepper, pour in enough oil to come almost to the top of the bowl, stir well, and set aside for at least 1 hour for the flavors to blend, or for up to 1 week in a covered jar in the refrigerator.

2. When ready to serve, heat a ridged grill pan over high heat. Working in batches, add as many pieces of bread as will fit in the pan in a single layer and brown for 3 minutes on each side, until marked with black lines and toasted. Alternatively, broil under a hot broiler until toasted.

3. Remove the bread slices from the pan and rub with the garlic halves, pressing down firmly, then brush with oil and sprinkle with salt. Set aside while you brown the remaining bread.

4. Cut each piece of toast into thirds and put on a serving platter. Stir the scallions into the olive mixture, then spoon the mixture into a serving bowl and serve with the pieces of toast.

Funghi Farciti
Creamy Stuffed Mushrooms

SERVES 4

1 ounce dried porcini
2 russet potatoes, diced
2 tablespoons melted butter
¼ cup heavy cream
2 tablespoons snipped fresh chives
8 portobello mushrooms
¼ cup shredded Swiss cheese
⅔ cup vegetable stock
salt and pepper, to taste

1. Preheat the oven to 425°F. Place the dried porcini in a small bowl. Add enough boiling water to cover and let soak for 20 minutes.

2. Meanwhile, cook the potatoes in a saucepan of lightly salted boiling water for 10 minutes, until cooked through and tender. Drain well and mash until smooth.

3. Drain the soaked porcini and then chop them finely. Mix them into the mashed potatoes.

4. Thoroughly blend together the butter, cream, and chives and pour into the potato mixture, mixing well. Season with salt and pepper.

5. Remove the stems from the portobello mushrooms. Chop the stems and stir them into the potato mixture. Spoon the mixture into the mushrooms and sprinkle the cheese over the top.

6. Arrange the stuffed mushrooms in a shallow baking dish and pour in the stock.

7. Cover the dish and cook in the preheated oven for 20 minutes. Uncover and cook for an additional 5 minutes, until golden. Serve the mushrooms immediately.

Insalata di Crudo, Salami & Fichi
Ham & Salami Salad with Figs

1. Trim the stems of the figs to leave just a short length, then cut the figs into quarters.

2. Arrange the ham and salami on a large serving platter.

3. Wash and dry the herbs and arugula and put in a bowl with the prepared figs.

4. Whisk together the lemon juice and oil in a small bowl and season well with salt and pepper. Pour the lemon juice-and-oil mixture into the bowl with the herbs, arugula, and figs. Toss carefully until all the ingredients are well coated in the dressing.

5. Spoon the figs and salad on top of the meat on the serving platter. Serve immediately.

SERVES 6

6 ripe figs
6 thin slices prosciutto
12 thin slices salami
1 small bunch of fresh
  basil, separated into
  small sprigs
a few fresh mint sprigs
handful of arugula
2 tablespoons lemon
  juice
¼ cup extra virgin
  olive oil
salt and pepper,
  to taste

Zucchini Fritti

Fried Zucchini

Menu

1. Heat the oil in a skillet over medium heat. Add the onion, reduce the heat to low, and sauté, stirring, for 5—8 minutes, until it is just starting to lightly brown. Stir in the garlic.

2. Add the zucchini and oregano and season with salt and pepper. Increase the heat to medium—high and sauté, turning over the zucchini slices occasionally, for 5—8 minutes, until just starting to become tender.

3. Add the tomato puree, bring to a boil, and cook, without stirring, until the zucchini are tender but not mushy. Adjust the seasoning, if necessary.

4. Transfer the zucchini to a warm serving dish and drizzle with a little oil. Set aside to cool and serve with slices of bread (if using).

SERVES 4

2 tablespoons olive oil, plus extra for drizzling
1 onion, finely chopped
2 large garlic cloves, minced
3 zucchini (about 1 pound), halved lengthwise and thinly sliced
½ teaspoon dried oregano
⅔ cup tomato puree or tomato sauce
salt and pepper, to taste
Italian bread slices, to serve (optional)

Minestrone
Minestrone

SERVES 6

2 tablespoons olive oil
1 large onion, chopped
2 garlic cloves, minced
2 celery stalks, chopped
½ small green cabbage, shredded
⅔ cup red wine
7 cups vegetable stock
¼ cup dried cannellini beans,
   soaked overnight, then rinsed
   and drained
4 plum tomatoes, peeled,
   seeded, and diced
2 tablespoons tomato paste
2 teaspoons sugar
2 carrots, diced
⅓ cup fresh shelled peas
½ cup green bean pieces
2 ounces dried soup pasta
2 tablespoons chopped fresh
   mixed herbs
salt and pepper, to taste
grated Parmesan cheese, to serve

1. Heat the oil in a large saucepan. Add the onion, garlic, and celery and cook over low heat, stirring occasionally, for 5—7 minutes, until the onion has softened. Stir in the cabbage and cook, stirring frequently, for an additional 5 minutes.

2 Increase the heat to medium, pour in the wine, and cook for about 2 minutes, until the alcohol has evaporated, then pour in the stock. Add the cannellini beans and bring to a boil, then reduce the heat, cover, and simmer for 2½ hours.

3. Add the tomatoes, tomato paste, sugar, carrots, peas, green beans, pasta, and herbs and season with salt and pepper. Simmer for 20—25 minutes, until the pasta is cooked and the vegetables are tender.

4. Ladle the soup into warm bowls and serve immediately with Parmesan cheese.

Tortelloni in Brodo

Pasta in Chicken Soup

1. Put the chicken, bay leaves, carrot, celery, onion, and 2 teaspoons of salt into a large stockpot or deep saucepan. Pour in the water to cover and slowly bring to just below boiling point, skimming the surface occasionally to remove the scum. Do not let the liquid boil.

2. Reduce the heat to low, cover, and let simmer for 1 hour. Skim the surface again, if necessary. Stir in the cheese rind, replace the lid, and simmer for an additional 20 minutes, until the chicken is cooked through. Or cook until the chicken is tender and the juices run clear when the tip of a knife is inserted into the thickest part of the meat. Remove the chicken pieces (and set aside if using for the main dish, see Mama's Tip on right). Remove and discard the cheese rind.

3. Strain the liquid into a large bowl, pressing down on the vegetables. Skim the surface, then transfer 5 cups of the broth to a large saucepan. Adjust the salt, if necessary, and add pepper.

4. Bring to a boil, add the tortelloni, and cook for 2 minutes, or according to the package directions, until they are al dente.

5. Ladle the pasta and broth into bowls and serve with Parmesan cheese for sprinkling (if using).

SERVES 4

1 oven-ready chicken, about
  3½ pounds, cut into pieces
  and skinned
2 bay leaves
1 large carrot, coarsely chopped
1 large celery stalk with
  leaves, coarsely chopped
1 large onion, unpeeled,
  cut into quarters
8¾ cups water
2-inch piece Parmesan
  cheese rind
10 ounces fresh tortelloni
salt and pepper, to taste
freshly grated Parmesan cheese,
  to serve (optional)

Mamá's Tip:
Canny Italian cooks turn this simple dish
into a two-course meal. Keep the chicken
hot and serve it as the main dish.

Zuppa di Pomodoro

Fresh Tomato Soup
with Pasta

SERVES 4

1 tablespoon olive oil
4 large plum tomatoes
1 onion, cut into quarters
1 garlic clove, thinly sliced
1 celery stalk, coarsely chopped
2 cups chicken stock
2 ounces dried soup pasta
salt and pepper, to taste
chopped fresh flat-leaf parsley,
    to garnish

1. Pour the oil into a large, heavy saucepan and add the tomatoes, onion, garlic, and celery. Cover and cook over low heat, occasionally shaking gently, for 45 minutes, until pulpy.

2. Transfer the mixture to a food processor or blender and process to a smooth puree.

3. Push the puree through a strainer into a clean saucepan.

4. Add the stock and bring to a boil. Add the pasta, bring back to a boil, and cook for 8—10 minutes, or according to the package directions, until the pasta is tender but still firm to the bite. Season with salt and pepper.

5. Ladle into warm bowls, sprinkle with parsley, and serve immediately.

Zuppa di Vongole
Clam Soup

1. Heat the oil in a large saucepan over medium heat. Add the fish heads, onion, carrot, celery, and fennel, reduce the heat to low, and simmer for 8 minutes. Add the garlic and simmer for an additional 2 minutes.

2. Stir in the wine, bring to a boil, and boil until reduced by half. Add the tomato puree, water, and crushed red pepper (if using), and season with salt and pepper. Bring to a boil, skimming the surface occasionally, then reduce the heat to low, cover, and simmer for 15 minutes.

3. Meanwhile, preheat the broiler to high. Rinse the clams in several changes of water until the water runs clear. Discard any with broken shells and any that refuse to close when tapped. Toast the bread on both sides under the preheated broiler.

SERVES 4

4 tablespoons olive oil
2 fish heads or ¾–1 pound
  fish trimmings
1 onion, chopped
1 carrot, finely diced
1 celery stalk, finely diced
1 fennel bulb, finely diced
2 large garlic cloves, chopped
1 cup dry white wine
3 cups tomato puree or
  tomato sauce
3 cups water
pinch of crushed red pepper
  (optional)
3 pounds scrubbed fresh clams
4 slices day-old Italian bread
4 tomatoes, seeded and diced
1 tablespoon finely chopped
  fresh mint
1 tablespoon finely chopped
  fresh dill
salt and pepper, to taste

4. Strain the soup through a strainer lined with cheesecloth, pressing down to extract as much flavor as possible. Transfer the strained liquid to a large saucepan and bring to a boil over high heat. Reduce the heat to low, add the clams, cover, and simmer for 3—5 minutes, until the clams have opened. Use a slotted spoon to remove and discard any clams that remain closed.

5. Stir in the tomatoes, mint, and dill and adjust the seasoning, if necessary. Simmer for an additional 2 minutes. Place a piece of bread in the bottom of four warm bowls, then ladle the clams and soup over them. Serve immediately.

Caponata
Italian Eggplants

SERVES 4

¼ cup olive oil
2 celery stalks, chopped
2 red onions, chopped
1 eggplant, diced
1 garlic clove, minced
5 plum tomatoes, chopped
3 tablespoons red wine
   vinegar
1 tablespoon sugar
¼ cup pitted green olives
2 tablespoons capers
¼ cup chopped fresh
   flat-leaf parsley
salt and pepper, to taste
ciabatta bread, to serve

1. Heat half of the oil in a large, heavy saucepan. Add the celery and onions and cook over low heat, stirring occasionally, for 5 minutes, until softened but not browned.

2. Add the remaining oil and the eggplant. Cook, stirring frequently, for about 5 minutes, until the eggplant starts to brown.

3. Add the garlic, tomatoes, vinegar, and sugar and mix well. Cover the mixture with a circle of wax paper and simmer gently for about 10 minutes.

4. Remove the wax paper, stir in the olives and capers, and season with salt and pepper. Pour into a serving dish and set aside to cool to room temperature.

5. When cool, sprinkle the parsley over the top. Serve immediately with ciabatta bread.

VENEZIA
ST MARK'S BASILICA

Perfetto Pizza
& Pasta

Ahh, *perfetto* pizza and pasta — the staple dishes of any Italian family cook! This is simple, wholesome, and delicious food, suitable for all ages, all walks of life, and for all times of the day. If the humblest peasant sweating in the vineyards of Calabria can sit down to Mushroom Pizza or Homemade Gnocchi & Walnut Pesto, then so can Il Primo Ministro and the dignitaries of Rome! You know, it is a source of mystery to me why people buy frozen pizza. I hear from my son Gianluca, who wears a suit and works in the city, that for some people today modern life can be busy and fast paced. Apparently, there is not always time to prepared homecooked meals … to which I say *nonsenso!* As this chapter shows, creating *perfetto* pizza and pasta is something everyone can do with ease and enjoyment.

Pizza alle Salsiccie

Italian Sausage Pizza

1. Put the onion into a nonmetallic bowl, sprinkle 2 teaspoons of salt over it, toss, and set aside for at least 20 minutes.

2. Meanwhile, preheat the oven to 425°F. Dust two large baking sheets with polenta and set aside.

3. Heat the oil in a large skillet over high heat. Add the sausage meat and cook, stirring, for 3—5 minutes, until cooked through. Transfer to a strainer and let drain.

4. Rinse the onion, then pat completely dry with paper towels and set aside.

5. Turn out the dough onto a lightly floured work surface and gently knead. Divide into four equal pieces and roll each piece into a ball. Work with one ball at a time, keeping the remainder covered.

6. Using a lightly floured rolling pin, roll out each ball of dough into a 9—10-inch circle and transfer to a prepared baking sheet. Spread one-quarter each of the sauce, sausage meat, onion, and cheese over each dough circle, then season with salt and pepper.

7. Bake the pizzas in the preheated oven for 15—18 minutes, until the crust is crisp and the cheese is melted and golden. Serve immediately.

MAKES 4

1 red onion, thinly sliced
fine polenta or all-purpose
  flour, for dusting
2 tablespoons olive oil
1 pound spicy or mild Italian
  sausages, casing removed and
  meat coarsely crumbled
1 quantity Pizza Dough
  (see page 45)
Italian 00 flour or all-purpose
  flour, for kneading
½ cup store-bought pizza sauce
⅔ cup freshly grated
  Parmesan cheese
salt and pepper, to taste

Mama's Tip:
For all my wisdom about how to create
the perfect pizza, read my advice on
pages 44 and 45.

Mama's tips for the perfect pizza

Nothing says Italian family food like pizza. I remember many summers ago my son Gianluca once tried to tell me we Italians actually took the recipe from the ancient Greeks. To this, I replied that pizza has been cooked in Mama's family for hundreds of years — if anything the ancient Greeks owe their food to my descendants and I don't care what the history books say!

And what's more, we've been making it the same way for pretty much all that time. Mama's basic pizza recipe is *molto facile* — and *molto delizioso*!

3⅔ cups Italian 00 or
    all-purpose flour, plus
    extra for dusting
2¼ teaspoons active dry yeast
1 teaspoon salt
1 tablespoon extra virgin olive
    oil, plus extra for the bowl
1-1¼ cups water, heated to 115°F

Mama's Basic Pizza Dough

1. Mix together the flour, yeast, and salt in a large bowl and make a well in the center. Add the oil and 1 cup of water and gradually stir in the flour from the side until a soft dough forms — caress the flour in, firmly but gently, like you're bathing a *bambino*. Add more water, if needed, to create a soft dough.

2. Turn out the dough onto a lightly floured surface and knead until smooth and elastic. You can be a little firmer now — show the dough that Mama is boss! Once you're happy, shape the dough into a ball.

3. Wash and dry the bowl, then lightly run the inside with oil. Add the dough and roll it around so it is lightly coated. Cover the bowl with plastic wrap and set aside in a warm place — Mama uses a corner of the kitchen, out of the sun but near the window — until the dough doubles in size, which can take up to 2 hours.

Use as directed in a recipe—but don't skimp on your toppings!

Pizza Fiorentina
Spinach & Olive Pizza

MAKES 2

fine polenta or all-purpose flour, for dusting
1½ (6-ounce) packages fresh spinach, washed and drained
½ quantity Pizza Dough (see page 45)
Italian 00 flour or all-purpose flour, for kneading
1 cup store-bought pizza sauce
2 garlic cloves, minced
¼ cup ripe black olives, pitted and halved
2 tablespoons garlic olive oil
2 eggs
1 cup finely grated Grana Padano cheese or Parmesan cheese
salt and pepper, to taste

1. Preheat the oven to 425°F. Dust a large baking sheet with polenta and set aside.

2. Put the spinach into a small saucepan, place over low heat, and cook for 1—2 minutes, or until it has wilted. Drain the spinach in a strainer, pressing down with the back of a spoon to remove any remaining water.

3. Turn out the dough onto a lightly floured work surface and gently knead. Divide into two equal pieces and roll each piece into a ball. Work with one ball at a time, keeping the other covered.

4. Using a lightly floured rolling pin, roll out each ball of dough into a 9—10-inch circle and transfer to the prepared baking sheet. Spread half of the sauce over each dough circle, then sprinkle each pizza with garlic. Top with the spinach and olives, drizzle with the garlic oil, and season with salt and pepper.

5. Bake in the preheated oven for 11—13 minutes, then remove from the oven and make a small indentation in the center of each pizza. Break an egg into each indentation and sprinkle the cheese on top. Return to the oven and bake for an additional 3—5 minutes, or until the eggs are just cooked and the crusts are crisp, and serve.

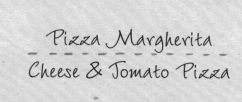

1. Preheat the oven to 425°F. Dust a large baking sheet with polenta and set aside.

2. Turn out the dough onto a lightly floured work surface and gently knead. Divide into two equal pieces and roll each piece into a ball. Work with one ball at a time, keeping the other covered.

3. Using a lightly floured rolling pin, roll out each ball of dough into a 9—10-inch circle and transfer to the prepared baking sheet.

4. Top each dough circle with the tomato and mozzarella slices. Season with salt and pepper, sprinkle with the basil, and drizzle with the oil.

5. Bake in the preheated oven for 15—18 minutes, or until the crust is crisp and the cheese is melted and golden.

6. Serve immediately.

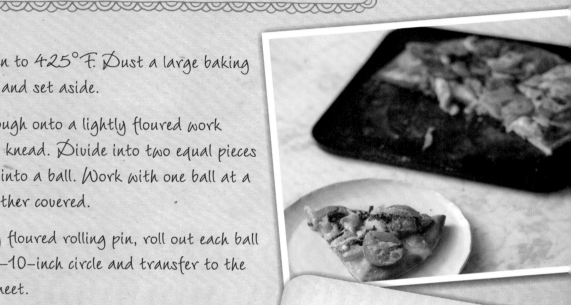

MAKES 2

fine polenta or all-purpose flour, for dusting
½ quantity Pizza Dough (see page 45)
Italian 00 flour or all-purpose flour, for kneading
6 tomatoes, thinly sliced
6 ounces mozzarella cheese, thinly sliced
2 tablespoons shredded fresh basil
2 tablespoons olive oil
salt and pepper, to taste

Pizza alle Verdure
Vegetable Pizza

1. Preheat a ridged grill pan over high heat. Brush the zucchini slices with oil, then add as many as will fit in the pan in a single layer and cook for 1—2 minutes on each side, until marked with black lines and heated through. Set aside and repeat with the remaining slices.

2. Meanwhile, preheat the oven to 425°F. Dust two large baking sheets with polenta and set aside.

3. Turn out the dough onto a lightly floured work surface and gently knead. Divide into four equal pieces and roll each piece into a ball. Work with one ball at a time, keeping the remainder covered.

4. Using a lightly floured rolling pin, roll out each ball of dough into a 9—10-inch circle and transfer to a prepared baking sheet.

MAKES 4

2 zucchini, halved lengthwise
  and thinly sliced into
  semicricles
1 tablespoon olive oil,
  plus extra if needed
fine polenta or all-purpose
  flour, for dusting
1 quantity Pizza Dough
  (see page 45)
Italian 00 flour or all-purpose
  flour, for kneading
½ cup store-bought pizza sauce
16 sun-dried tomatoes in oil,
  drained and quartered
2 teaspoons dried dill
⅔ cup crumbled soft goat
  cheese
salt and pepper, to taste

Mama's Tip:
Sprinkle a handful of pitted
ripe black olives over the
pizza before cooking it—they
are a perfect pairing with the
goat cheese.

5. Spread one-quarter of the sauce over each dough circle, followed by one-quarter each of the zucchini slices, tomatoes, dill, and cheese. Season with salt and pepper.

6. Bake the pizzas in the preheated oven for 15—18 minutes, until the crust is crisp and the cheese is melted and golden. Serve immediately.

Pizza ai Gamberi
Seafood Pizza

MAKES 2

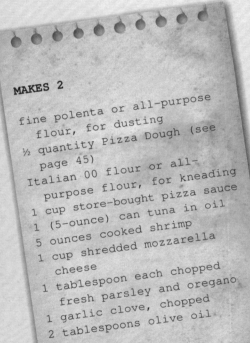

fine polenta or all-purpose flour, for dusting
½ quantity Pizza Dough (see page 45)
Italian 00 flour or all-purpose flour, for kneading
1 cup store-bought pizza sauce
1 (5-ounce) can tuna in oil
5 ounces cooked shrimp
1 cup shredded mozzarella cheese
1 tablespoon each chopped fresh parsley and oregano
1 garlic clove, chopped
2 tablespoons olive oil

1. Preheat the oven to 425°F. Dust a large baking sheet with polenta and set aside.

2. Turn out the dough onto a lightly floured work surface and gently knead. Divide into two equal pieces and roll each piece into a ball. Work with one ball at a time, keeping the other covered.

3. Using a lightly floured rolling pin, roll out each ball of dough into a 9—10-inch circle and transfer to the prepared baking sheet.

4. Top each dough circle with the pizza sauce. Coarsely flake the tuna and spread it over each pizza, then arrange the shrimp on top. Sprinkle with the mozzarella.

5. Mix together the parsley, oregano, garlic, and olive oil, and drizzle the mixture over the pizzas.

6. Bake in the preheated oven for about 15—18 minutes, or until the crust is crisp and the cheese is melted and golden. Serve immediately.

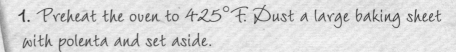

Calzone ai Tonno e Peperoni Rossi
Tuna & Red Pepper Calzone

MAKES 4

fine polenta or all-purpose
   flour, for dusting
1 quantity Pizza Dough
   (see page 45)
Italian 00 flour or all-purpose
   flour, for kneading
½ cup store-bought pizza sauce
1 (12-ounce) can tuna in olive
   oil, drained and flaked
12 roasted red peppers in
   olive oil, drained and sliced,
   oil reserved
1 cup sliced, pitted ripe
   black olives
salt and pepper, to taste

1. Preheat the oven to 425°F. Dust a large baking sheet with polenta and set aside.

2. Turn out the dough onto a lightly floured work surface and gently knead. Divide into four equal pieces and roll each piece into a ball. Work with one ball at a time, keeping the remainder covered.

3. Using a lightly floured rolling pin, roll each ball of dough into a 9—10-inch circle. Spread one-quarter of the sauce over half of the dough circle, leaving a ½-inch border. Add one-quarter of the tuna, then top with one-quarter each of the roasted red peppers and olives. Season with salt and pepper.

4. Fold the uncovered half of the dough over the filling and securely fold the edge in on itself. Be careful to seal tightly, so the calzone doesn't split while baking, letting the filling seep out.

5. Gently transfer the calzone to the prepared baking sheet and cover with a dish towel while you prepare the remaining calzones.

6. Lightly brush the tops of the calzones with some of the reserved oil from the roasted peppers. Bake in the preheated oven for 15—18 minutes, until puffed and golden brown. Let cool for a few minutes, then serve.

Pizza Capricciosa

Capricciosa Pizza

MAKES 2

fine polenta or all-purpose flour,
  for dusting
½ quantity Pizza Dough (see
  page 45)
Italian 00 flour or all-purpose
  flour, for kneading
1 cup store-bought pizza sauce
8 ounces Italian salami,
  thinly sliced
1 orange bell pepper, seeded and
  finely sliced
4 artichoke hearts in vegetable oil,
  drained and cut into quarters
½ teaspoon dried oregano
6 ounces soft goat cheese,
  thinly sliced
salt and pepper, to taste

1. Preheat the oven to 425°F. Dust a large baking sheet with polenta and set aside.

2. Turn out the dough onto a lightly floured work surface and gently knead. Divide into two equal pieces and roll each piece into a ball. Work with one ball at a time, keeping the other covered.

3. Using a lightly floured rolling pin, roll out each ball of dough into a 9—10-inch circle and transfer to the prepared baking sheet.

4. Top each dough circle with the pizza sauce, and spread it almost to the edges. Sprinkle with the salami, orange bell pepper, artichoke hearts, and oregano, then top with the cheese. Season with salt and pepper.

5. Bake in the preheated oven for 15—18 minutes, or until the crust is crisp and the cheese is melted and golden. Serve immediately.

Pizza ai Funghi

Mushroom Pizza

1. Preheat the oven to 425°F. Dust two large baking sheets with polenta and set aside.

2. Heat the oil in a large skillet over medium—high heat. Add the mushrooms, thyme, and crushed red pepper (if using). Sprinkle with salt and sauté, stirring, for 5—8 minutes, until the mushrooms are tender and reabsorb the liquid they release.

3. Turn out the dough onto a lightly floured work surface and gently knead. Divide into four equal pieces and roll each piece into a ball. Work with one ball at a time, keeping the remainder covered.

4. Using a lightly floured rolling pin, roll each ball of dough into a 9—10-inch circle and transfer to a prepared baking sheet. Using a slotted spoon, transfer one-quarter of the mushroom mixture to each dough circle, draining off as much oil as possible. Spread out to cover the surface. Sprinkle with the cheese and season with salt and pepper.

5. Bake in the preheated oven for 15—18 minutes, until the crust is crisp and the cheese is melted and golden. Serve immediately.

MAKES 4

fine polenta or all-purpose
  flour, for dusting
2 tablespoons olive oil
1¾ pounds portobello mushrooms,
  thinly sliced
leaves from 4 fresh thyme
  sprigs, or 1 tablespoon
  dried thyme
½ teaspoon crushed red pepper
  (optional)
1 quantity Pizza Dough
  (see page 45)
Italian 00 flour or all-purpose
  flour, for kneading
12 ounces Taleggio cheese,
  rinded and thinly sliced
salt and pepper, to taste

Mama's Tip:
For a delicious garlic flavor, use
garlic oil to sauté the mushrooms,
and drizzle some over the pizza after
it is cooked.

Pizza ai Carciofi
Artichoke Pizza

MAKES 4

fine polenta or all-purpose
   flour, for dusting
1 quantity Pizza Dough
   (see page 45)
Italian 00 flour or all-purpose
   flour, for kneading
1 (14-ounce) can artichoke hearts
   in oil
8 mild whole chiles in oil
4 garlic cloves, minced
2 tablespoons finely chopped
   fresh flat-leaf parsley
¼ cup olive oil
1½ cups diced mozzarella cheese
salt and pepper, to taste

1. Preheat the oven to 425°F. Dust two large baking sheets with polenta and set aside.

2. Turn out the dough onto a lightly floured work surface and gently knead. Divide into four equal pieces and roll each piece into a ball. Work with one ball at a time, keeping the remainder covered.

3. Using a lightly floured rolling pin, roll out each ball of dough into a 9—10-inch circle and transfer to a prepared baking sheet.

4. Slice the artichoke hearts lengthwise. Sprinkle the artichokes and chiles on top of each dough circle. Sprinkle with garlic and half of the parsley. Season with salt and pepper and drizzle the olive oil on top. Put the mozzarella on top of the pizzas and bake for about 15—18 minutes. Sprinkle with the remaining parsley before serving.

Ziti al Forno
Baked Ziti

1. Preheat the oven to 425°F. Lightly grease a large baking dish with oil.

2. Bring a large saucepan of lightly salted water to a boil. Add the ziti, bring back to a boil, and cook for 2 minutes less than specified in the package directions.

3. Meanwhile, beat together the ricotta cheese, half of the mozzarella cheese, and one-third of the Parmesan cheese in a large bowl. Season with salt and pepper and set aside.

4. Just before the pasta finishes cooking, take ¼ cup of the pasta cooking liquid and beat into the cheese mixture until a creamy sauce starts to form.

5. Drain the pasta, add it to the bowl, and stir until coated with cheese. Stir in the tomato sauce, parsley, and crushed red pepper (if using), and stir until well mixed.

6. Transfer the pasta to the prepared baking dish and smooth the surface. Sprinkle the remaining mozzarella cheese and Parmesan cheese over the dish.

7. Place the dish on a baking sheet and bake in the preheated oven for 25—30 minutes, until golden brown on top. Let stand for a few minutes, then serve straight from the dish.

SERVES 4

olive oil, for greasing
1 pound dried ziti or penne
1 cup ricotta cheese
2 cups shredded mozzarella
   cheese
1 cup freshly grated
   Parmesan cheese
3 cups tomato pasta sauce
   with herbs
2 tablespoons chopped fresh
   parsley
pinch of crushed red pepper
   (optional)
salt and pepper, to taste

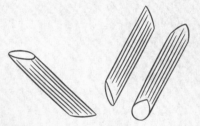

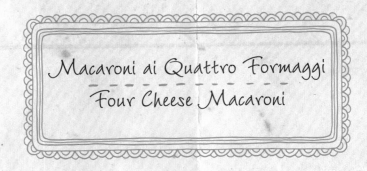

Macaroni ai Quattro Formaggi
Four Cheese Macaroni

1. Preheat the oven to 400°F. Lightly grease a large baking dish with butter, then set aside. Mix one-third of the Parmesan cheese with the bread crumbs and set aside.

2. Bring a large saucepan of lightly salted water to a boil, add the macaroni, bring back to a boil, and cook for 2 minutes less than specified in the package directions. Drain well, rinse with cold water, drain again, and set aside.

3. Meanwhile, melt the butter in a saucepan over medium heat. Sprinkle the flour on top and stir for 2 minutes, until blended. Remove the pan from the heat and stir in the milk, stirring continuously to prevent lumps from forming.

SERVES 4

1 cup freshly grated
 Parmesan cheese
1 cup fine dry bread crumbs
1 pound dried macaroni
3 tablespoons butter, plus
 extra for greasing
⅓ cup all-purpose flour
2 cups lukewarm milk
freshly grated nutmeg,
 to taste
¾ cup finely chopped Gorgonzola
 cheese
¾ cup shredded provolone or
 Taleggio cheese
½ cup diced mozzarella cheese
olive oil, for drizzling
salt and pepper, to taste

4. Return the pan to the heat, stir in the nutmeg, and season with salt and pepper. Slowly bring to a boil, stirring, until the sauce thickens. Stir in the remaining Parmesan cheese, the Gorgonzola cheese, and the provolone cheese and continue stirring until the cheeses melt and blend. Stir in the mozzarella cheese.

5. Add the macaroni and stir to coat in the sauce. Adjust the seasoning, if necessary. Transfer the mixture to the prepared dish and smooth the surface. Sprinkle the bread crumb mixture over the top and drizzle with oil.

6. Place the dish on a baking sheet and bake in the preheated oven for 20—25 minutes, until golden brown on top. Let stand for a few minutes, then serve straight from the dish.

Ravioli Classici
Classic Ravioli

1. To make the filling, put the bread crumbs and milk into a bowl and set aside to soak. Roll the dough into eight balls and wrap in plastic wrap.

2. Heat the oil in a large skillet over medium heat. Add the shallot and stir for 1—2 minutes, or until beginning to soften. Stir in the beef, pork, garlic, prosciutto, and sage and season with salt and pepper. Stir for an additional 2—4 minutes, breaking up the meat until it is brown all over. Stir in the bread crumbs. Add the wine, bring to a boil, and boil, stirring, until it has just evaporated. Stir in the cheese.

3. Lightly dust a work surface and a baking sheet with semolina. Roll one dough ball into a strip about 4 inches wide and 20 inches long, as described on page 67, and lay it on the work surface.

4. Use a 3-inch round cutter to cut out 6—8 circles. Place 1 teaspoon of filling slightly off center on each. Rub water around the edge of each circle, then gently fold over the top half and press to seal. Use the tines of a fork to press all around.

5. Transfer to the prepared baking sheet and cover. Repeat with the remaining dough, rerolling the scraps, until all the filling has been used. Let rest for at least 1 hour, or cover and chill for up to 24 hours.

6. Bring a large saucepan of lightly salted water to a boil, add the ravioli, bring back to a boil, and cook for 2 minutes, until tender. Use a slotted spoon to transfer the ravioli to a warm serving dish. Drizzle with oil and sprinkle with salt and pepper. Serve with Parmesan cheese.

SERVES 4

1 quantity Pasta Dough, rested
   but not rolled, (see page 66)
fine semolina, for dusting
olive oil, to serve
salt and pepper, to taste

FILLING
⅓ cup fresh white bread crumbs
1 tablespoon milk
1 tablespoon olive oil
1 shallot, finely chopped
4 ounces fresh ground beef
4 ounces fresh ground pork
2 garlic cloves, minced
2 slices prosciutto,
   finely chopped
½ teaspoon dried sage or thyme
¼ cup red wine
⅓ cup finely grated fresh
   Parmesan cheese, plus extra
   to serve
salt and pepper, to taste

Mamá's Tip:
For advice on making your own
pasta dough, see pages 66 and 67.

Making your own delicious pasta

Now I am going to teach you my basic ravioli dough recipe. Lucky for you, it's molto facile!

MAKES ENOUGH FOR 4

1⅔ cups Italian 00 or
   all-purpose flour, plus
   extra for kneading and dusting
½ teaspoon salt
2 eggs, beaten
2 teaspoons olive oil
fine semolina, for dusting

Mama's Basic Ravioli Dough

1. Sift the flour and salt together into a large bowl, then make a well in the center. Add the eggs and oil and gradually stir together with a fork until the liquid has been absorbed. Use your hands to knead the mixture in the bowl, firmly and gently, sprinkling in water, if necessary, until a dough forms.

2. Turn out the dough onto a lightly floured surface and knead until it becomes smooth and elastic. Shape the dough into a ball.

3. Wash and dry the bowl. Add the ball of dough, cover with plastic wrap, and let rest for at least 30 minutes.

4. Cut the dough into eight equal pieces and roll into balls. Work with one ball of dough at a time, keeping the remaining balls covered to prevent them from drying out.

5. Set the pasta machine to 0 and dust the rollers with flour. Use your palm to flatten a dough ball. With steady hands, feed it through the machine, then fold each end into the center and feed it through again with the open ends at top and bottom. Repeat twice.

6. Switch the machine to setting 1 and roll the pasta through it, gently lifting and pulling the strip of pasta as it comes out of the machine. Continue feeding the pasta through the machine, changing the setting each time until you reach setting 5.

7. Lightly dust a clean surface with fine semolina. Lay the pasta on top, trim to size, and cover with a clean dish towel. Repeat with the remaining balls of pasta. Cut and fill the ravioli as on page 64 (or with any filling of your choosing).

Bene! Mama's delizioso pasta dough!

Lasagne ai Pollo & Funghi

Chicken & Mushroom Lasagna

1. Preheat the oven to 375°F. For the white sauce, heat the milk, butter, flour, and bay leaf in a saucepan over low heat, whisking continuously, until smooth and thick. Season with salt and pepper, cover, and let stand.

2. Heat the oil in a large saucepan over medium heat and sauté the onion, stirring, for 3—4 minutes.

3. Add the chicken and pancetta and cook for 6—8 minutes. Stir in both types of mushrooms and cook for an additional 2—3 minutes.

4. Add the wine and bring to a boil. Pour in the tomatoes, cover, and simmer for 20 minutes. Stir in the basil.

5. Meanwhile, bring a large saucepan of lightly salted water to a boil. Add the lasagna noodles, bring back to a boil, and cook according to the package directions. Drain well on a clean dish towel.

6. Spoon one-third of the meat sauce into a large baking dish. Remove and discard the bay leaf from the white sauce. Spoon one-quarter of the white sauce over the meat sauce. Arrange three of the lasagna noodles over the white sauce. Repeat the layers twice, finishing with a layer of white sauce.

7. Sprinkle with the Parmesan and bake in the preheated oven for 35—40 minutes, until the topping is golden brown and bubbling. Serve immediately.

SERVES 4

2 tablespoons olive oil
1 large onion, finely chopped
1 pound fresh ground chicken
4 ounces pancetta, chopped
3½ cups chopped cremini
  mushrooms
4 ounces dried porcini, soaked
⅔ cup dry white wine
1 (14½-ounce) can diced tomatoes
3 tablespoons chopped fresh
  basil
9 dried lasagna noodles
¼ cup finely grated Parmesan
  cheese

WHITE SAUCE
2½ cups milk
4 tablespoons butter
½ cup all-purpose flour
1 bay leaf
salt and pepper, to taste

Mama's Tip:
If you don't have ground chicken, you
can either make your own by putting
some chicken meat in a food processor
or buy ground turkey instead.

Linguine alla Puttanesca
Anchovy Linguine

SERVES 4

3 tablespoons olive oil
2 garlic cloves, finely chopped
10 anchovy fillets, chopped
1½ cups chopped, pitted ripe
    black olives
1 tablespoon capers
8 plum tomatoes, peeled, seeded,
    and chopped
cayenne pepper, to taste
1 pound dried linguine
salt, to taste
2 tablespoons chopped fresh
    flat-leaf parsley, to garnish

1. Heat the oil in a heavy saucepan. Add the garlic and cook over low heat, stirring frequently, for 2 minutes. Mash the anchovies to a pulp with a fork and add them to the pan.

2. Add the olives, capers, and tomatoes and season with cayenne pepper. Cover and simmer for 25 minutes.

3. Meanwhile, bring a saucepan of lightly salted water to a boil. Add the pasta, bring back to a boil, and cook according to the package directions, until tender but still firm to the bite.

4. Drain the pasta and transfer to a warm serving dish. Spoon the anchovy sauce into the dish and toss the pasta, using two large forks, until well coated. Garnish with parsley and serve immediately.

Fettucine Alfredo
Fettucine Alfredo

SERVES 4

1 pound dried fettucine
6 tablespoons unsalted butter,
    diced
2 garlic cloves, minced
1¾ cups heavy cream
2 cups freshly grated Parmesan
    cheese, plus extra to serve
    (optional)
salt and pepper, to taste

1. Bring a large saucepan of lightly salted water to a boil. Add the pasta, bring back to a boil, and cook according to the package directions, until tender but still firm to the bite.

2. Meanwhile, melt the butter in a large skillet over medium heat. Add the garlic and stir for 1 minute, being careful that it doesn't brown. Stir in the cream and bring to a boil. Add half of the cheese and stir until melted, then reduce the heat to low and season with salt and pepper.

3. Drain the pasta without shaking and reserve a little of the cooking liquid. Immediately add the hot pasta and the remaining cheese to the cream sauce, using two forks to toss until well coated. If the sauce seems too thick, add a little of the reserved cooking liquid to thin it, then toss again.

4. Divide among warm bowls and serve immediately, with extra cheese (if using).

Rigatoni ai Zucchini
Roast Zucchini Rigatoni

SERVES 4

4 zucchini, chopped
2½ tablespoons olive oil
1 onion, finely chopped
1 garlic clove, crushed
1 (28-ounce) can diced tomatoes
6 sun-dried tomatoes, chopped
1 cup vegetable stock
½ teaspoon dried oregano
12 ounces dried rigatoni
½ cup mascarpone cheese
salt and pepper, to taste
large handful of fresh basil
leaves, torn into pieces

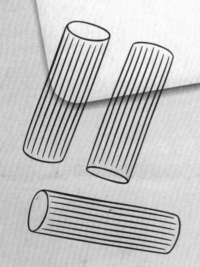

1. Preheat the oven to 400°F. Place the zucchini and 1½ tablespoons of the oil in a large baking dish. Toss together and spread out in a single layer. Roast in the preheated oven for 15—20 minutes, until tender and lightly browned.

2. Meanwhile, heat the remaining oil in a saucepan. Add the onion and garlic and cook over low heat for 5 minutes, until soft. Add the canned tomatoes, sun-dried tomatoes, stock, and oregano. Simmer for 10 minutes, until the liquid has reduced slightly.

3. Bring a large saucepan of lightly salted water to a boil. Add the rigatoni, bring back to a boil, and cook according to the package directions, or until tender but still firm to the bite. Drain well, then return to the pan.

4. Add the mascarpone cheese to the hot sauce and stir until melted and smooth. Season well with salt and pepper. Add to the pasta with the roasted zucchini and the basil leaves. Toss together until the pasta is well coated in sauce. Serve immediately.

SERVES 2

8 ounces dried penne
1 tablespoon olive oil
2 skinless, boneless chicken
  breasts
¼ cup dry white wine
¾ cup frozen peas
⅓ cup heavy cream
salt, to taste
¼–⅓ cup chopped fresh flat-leaf
  parsley, to garnish

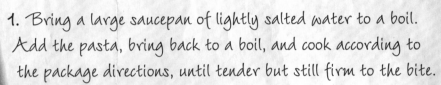

1. Bring a large saucepan of lightly salted water to a boil. Add the pasta, bring back to a boil, and cook according to the package directions, until tender but still firm to the bite.

2. Meanwhile, heat the oil in a skillet. Add the chicken and cook over medium heat for about 4 minutes on each side.

3. Pour in the wine and cook over high heat until it has almost evaporated.

4. Drain the pasta. Add the peas, cream, and pasta to the skillet, and stir well. Cover and simmer for 2 minutes.

5. Garnish the chicken-and-pasta mixture with parsley and serve immediately.

Mama's Tip:
Add a ¼ teaspoon of crushed red pepper with 1 (14-ounce) can tomatoes to add a little more depth to the sauce.

bianco

**Cannelloni di Spinaci
e Ricotta**

- - - - - - - - - - -

**Spinach & Ricotta
Cannelloni**

1. Preheat the oven to 350°F. Grease a large baking dish with the melted butter.

2. Bring a large saucepan of lightly salted water to a boil. Add the cannelloni tubes, bring back to a boil, and cook for 6—8 minutes, until nearly tender. Drain and rinse, then spread out on a clean dish towel.

3. For the filling, put the spinach and ricotta into a food processor and process briefly until combined. Add the egg and pecorino and process to a smooth paste. Transfer to a bowl, add the nutmeg, and season with salt and pepper.

4. Spoon the filling into a pastry bag fitted with a ½-inch tip. Carefully open a cannelloni tube and pipe in a little of the filling. Place the filled tube in the prepared dish and repeat.

5. For the cheese sauce, melt the butter in a saucepan. Add the flour to the butter and cook over low heat, stirring continuously, for 1 minute.

6. Remove from the heat and gradually stir in the hot milk. Return to the heat and bring to a boil, stirring continuously. Simmer over low heat, stirring frequently, for 10 minutes, until thickened and smooth.

7. Remove from the heat, stir in the Gruyère and season with salt and pepper.

8. Spoon the cheese sauce over the filled cannelloni. Cover the dish with aluminum foil and bake in the preheated oven for 20—25 minutes. Serve immediately.

SERVES 4

melted butter, for greasing
12 dried cannelloni tubes,
  each about 3 inches long
salt and pepper, to taste

FILLING
½ (10-ounce) package frozen
  spinach, thawed and drained
½ cup ricotta cheese
1 egg
¼ cup grated pecorino cheese
pinch of freshly grated nutmeg

CHEESE SAUCE
2 tablespoons butter
2 tablespoons all-purpose
  flour
2½ cups hot milk
¾ cup shredded Gruyère cheese
  or cheddar cheese

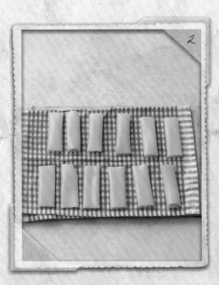

Gnocchi con Tacchino & Broccoli
Turkey & Broccoli Gnocchi

SERVES 4

1 tablespoon sunflower oil
1 pound turkey strips
2 small leeks, sliced diagonally
1 pound store-bought
    fresh gnocchi
3 cups broccoli florets
⅓ cup crème fraîche or plain
    yogurt
1 tablespoon whole-grain mustard
3 tablespoons orange juice
salt and pepper, to taste
¼ cup toasted pine nuts,
    to serve

1. Heat the oil in a large skillet. Add the turkey and leeks and cook over high heat for 5—6 minutes.

2. Meanwhile, bring a saucepan of lightly salted water to a boil. Add the gnocchi and broccoli, then cook for 3—4 minutes or according to the package directions.

3. Drain the gnocchi and broccoli and stir into the turkey mixture.

4. Mix together the crème fraîche, mustard, and orange juice in a small bowl. Season with salt and pepper, then stir into the pan. Serve immediately, sprinkled with pine nuts.

Gnocchi con Sugo di Noce
Homemade Gnocchi & Walnut Pesto

1. Cook the potatoes in their skins in a large saucepan of boiling water for 30—35 minutes, until tender. Drain well and let cool slightly.

2. Meanwhile, put all of the pesto ingredients in a food processor or blender and process for 2 minutes.

3. When the potatoes are cool enough to handle, peel off their skins and pass the flesh through a strainer into a large bowl or press through a potato ricer. Season well with salt and pepper and add the Parmesan. Beat in the egg and sift in the flour.

4. Lightly mix together, then turn out onto a lightly floured work surface. Knead lightly to form a smooth dough. If it is too sticky, add a little more flour.

5. Roll out the dough into a long log. Cut into 1-inch pieces and press with a fork to create the traditional ridged effect. Transfer to a floured baking sheet and cover with a dish towel.

6. Bring a large saucepan of water to a boil, add the gnocchi, and cook for 1—2 minutes. Remove with a slotted spoon and serve immediately with the walnut pesto.

SERVES 4

4 Yukon gold potatoes
¾ cup freshly grated Parmesan cheese
1 egg, beaten
1⅓ cups all-purpose flour, plus extra for dusting
salt and pepper, to taste

WALNUT PESTO
¾ cup fresh flat-leaf parsley leaves
2 tablespoons capers
2 garlic cloves, crushed
¾ cup extra virgin olive oil
½ cup chopped walnuts
½ cup freshly grated pecorino or Parmesan cheese

Dinner at Casa di Mama is always an event. Even the simplest meals are a family affair, a coming together at the end of the day to give thanks for all we have — even if sometimes it can seem like all we have is each other. There are some evenings where I'm just putting together the simplest frittata for myself and Alberto. On other evenings, I could be preparing a hearty vegetable stew for Marco, Filippo, their wives, and their *bambini*, or even celebrating a visit by the *nipoti* and *pronipoti* with something extra special, such as Baked Oregano Lobster. Whatever the occasion, dinners are the heart and soul of the family cook. It is at dinner — this most everyday of meals — that a family cook shows what she is really made of. And I should know: After all, I've raised a family of 40 on Mama's dinners!

Pollo alla Parmigiana
Chicken Parmesan

1. To make the sauce, heat the oil in a large saucepan. Add the onion and sauté, stirring, for 2 minutes. Add the garlic and cook, stirring, until the onion is soft. Stir in the herbs, tomatoes, tomato puree, oregano, and sugar and season with salt and pepper. Bring to a boil, cover, and simmer for 15 minutes. Transfer to a blender or food processor and puree.

2. Meanwhile, preheat the oven to 400°F. Spread the flour over a plate. Beat the eggs in a wide bowl, and put the bread crumbs on another plate. Halve the chicken breasts horizontally.

3. Place the chicken pieces between sheets of plastic wrap and pound with a meat mallet or rolling pin until about ¼ inch thick. Season both sides with salt and pepper. Dust a chicken breast with flour, shaking off the excess, then dip in the egg to coat. Dip in the bread crumbs to coat both sides, then set aside and repeat with the remaining chicken pieces.

4. Heat the oil in a skillet over medium—high heat. Add as many chicken pieces as will fit in the skillet in a single layer and cook on each side for 2 minutes, until golden. Drain on paper towels. Cook the remaining pieces, adding extra oil, if necessary. Pour half of the sauce into a baking dish that will hold the chicken in a single layer. Arrange the chicken on top, then pour over the remaining sauce. Arrange the mozzarella on top and sprinkle with the Parmesan cheese. Bake in the preheated oven for 20—25 minutes, or until the cheese is melted, golden, and bubbling. Let stand for 5 minutes, then garnish with parsley and serve immediately.

SERVES 4

¾ cup all-purpose flour
2 eggs
2 cups dry bread crumbs
4 skinless, boneless chicken
  breasts
about 2 tablespoons olive oil
9 ounces mozzarella, sliced
1½ cups freshly grated Parmesan
salt and pepper, to taste
chopped fresh flat-leaf
  parsley, to garnish

SIMPLE MARINARA SAUCE
2 tablespoons olive oil
1 large onion, chopped
2 large garlic cloves, chopped
1 tablespoon dried mixed herbs
1 (28-ounce) can diced tomatoes
1 cup tomato puree or
  tomato sauce
2 teaspoons dried oregano
pinch of sugar
salt and pepper, to taste

Polpettine con Ripieno di Mozzarella
Mozzarella-Stuffed Meatballs

1. Mix together the bread crumbs and milk in a bowl and set aside while you assemble the other ingredients.

2. Put the beef, Parmesan cheese, garlic, egg, grated onion, parsley, basil, mixed herbs, and salt and pepper in a bowl. Add the bread crumb mixture and use your hands to mix together.

3. Wet your hands and shape the mixture into 12 equal balls. Use your finger to make an indentation in the center of each ball, push in a cube of mozzarella cheese, and reroll the meat into a smooth ball. Make sure the seam is sealed, so that the melting cheese doesn't leak out during cooking. At this point, the meatballs can be covered and chilled for up to 12 hours. Return to room temperature before frying.

SERVES 4

¾ cup fine dry bread crumbs
2 tablespoons milk
1¼ pounds fresh ground beef
1¼ cup finely grated Parmesan
  cheese, plus extra for serving
2 large garlic cloves, minced
1 egg, beaten
3 onions, 1 grated and
  2 thinly sliced
2 tablespoons finely chopped
  fresh flat-leaf parsley
1 tablespoon finely chopped fresh
  basil, plus extra to garnish
1 teaspoon dried mixed herbs
4 ounces mozzarella, cut
  into twelve ½-inch cubes
2 tablespoons olive oil, plus
  extra for frying
2 cups tomato puree or
  tomato sauce
pinch of sugar
salt and pepper, to taste

4. Heat a thin layer of oil in a large skillet. Add as many meatballs as will fit in the skillet and cook for 3—5 minutes, until brown all over. Set aside and keep warm while cooking the remaining meatballs.

5. Heat 2 tablespoons of oil in a large saucepan or casserole dish. Stir in the sliced onions, reduce the heat to low, and sauté, stirring, for 5—8 minutes, until golden brown. Add the tomato puree and sugar and season with salt and pepper. Stir in the meatballs.

6. Bring to a boil, then reduce the heat, cover, and simmer for 20—25 minutes, or until the meatballs are cooked through when you cut one open. Adjust the seasoning of the sauce, if necessary. Serve immediately on warm plates, sprinkled with Parmesan cheese.

Mama's guide to setting an Italian dinner table

In Apulia, we don't stand on ceremony. I hear that, in certain wealthy establishments, dinners can be molto formale affairs, with many strict rules, such as which fork to use and when ... Not at Mama's table!

Mama believes a big family meal should, most of all, be an enjoyable experience — otherwise, what is the point? If everyone is worried about breaking some silly rule of etiquette, nobody relaxes ... and if nobody relaxes, nobody has a good time.

You need some rules, of course: Mama insists on everyone sitting to eat, and once you're seated at my table, you follow the law of my table — but don't worry. My rules are made to enhance the experience, not stifle it!

So ... here are Mama's rules for setting the table for a family meal.

Keep it simple. Plain tablecloths, napkins ... everything should be easily wipeable and washable. Big dinners mean spilled food — it's *naturale*!

Place plenty of water pitchers at intervals down the table — and keep enough wine out for guests to help themselves.

Bread and olives should also be set out on a help-yourself basis — I like a few big bowls in the middle of the table.

Mama sits at the head of the table — and Alberto always takes the other end. We are the hosts, and it is our job to keep the food, the vino, and the conversation flowing!

And remember — *piu importante*: a family meal is about having a good time above all else!

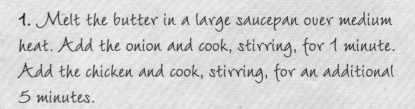

Risotto con Pollo
Chicken Risotto

SERVES 4

4 tablespoons butter
1 onion, chopped
5 ounces skinless, boneless
    chicken breasts, chopped
1¾ cups risotto rice
1 teaspoon ground turmeric
1¼ cups dry white wine
5 cups chicken stock,
    plus extra if needed
1 cup sliced cremini mushrooms
½ cup cashew nut halves
salt and pepper, to taste
Parmesan cheese shavings and
    fresh basil leaves,
    to garnish

1. Melt the butter in a large saucepan over medium heat. Add the onion and cook, stirring, for 1 minute. Add the chicken and cook, stirring, for an additional 5 minutes.

2. Add the rice and stir over medium heat for 1 minute, without browning. Add the turmeric and mix well.

3. Gradually stir in the wine, then stir in the stock, a ladleful at a time, waiting for each ladleful to be absorbed before stirring in the next.

4. Simmer for 20 minutes, stirring from time to time, until the rice is tender and nearly all of the liquid has been absorbed. If necessary, add a little more stock to prevent the risotto from drying out.

5. Stir in the mushrooms and cashew nuts, and cook for an additional 3 minutes. Season with salt and pepper.

6. Remove from the heat and spoon the mixture into warm serving dishes. Sprinkle with the Parmesan shavings and basil leaves and serve immediately.

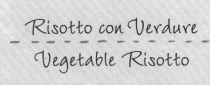

Risotto con Verdure
Vegetable Risotto

1. Heat the butter and olive oil in a large saucepan and sauté the onion, stirring, for 3—4 minutes, until softened.

2. Add the rice and stir over medium heat for 1 minute, without browning.

3. Add the wine and boil rapidly, stirring, until almost all evaporated.

4. Stir the stock into the pan, a ladleful at a time, allowing each ladleful to be absorbed before adding more.

5. After 15 minutes, add the asparagus and continue cooking, adding stock when necessary.

6. After an additional 5 minutes, stir in the walnuts and lemon rind, then adjust the seasoning, adding salt and pepper, if necessary.

7. Remove from the heat and drizzle with a little walnut oil, if using, stirring in lightly. Spoon the risotto into warm serving dishes and serve immediately, garnished with strips of lemon zest.

SERVES 4

1 tablespoon butter
3 tablespoons olive oil
1 small onion, finely chopped
1¾ cups risotto rice
⅔ cup dry white wine
6 cups vegetable stock
8 ounces asparagus tips,
  cut into 2½-inch lengths
⅓ cup chopped walnuts
grated rind of 1 lemon
salt and pepper, to taste
walnut oil, to serve
  (optional)
strips of lemon zest,
  to garnish

Rollatini
Eggplant Rollatini

1. Preheat the oven to 450°F. Place the eggplant slices in a single layer on a baking sheet, lightly brush with oil, and sprinkle with salt and pepper.

2. Place in the preheated oven and bake for 8—10 minutes, until tender. Remove from the oven and set aside. Reduce the oven temperature to 425°F.

3. Spread a thin layer of sauce in the bottom of a baking dish large enough to hold eight eggplant rolls in a single layer, then set aside.

4. Put the ricotta cheese, goat cheese, basil, and lemon rind in a bowl. Season with salt and pepper and beat together until smooth. Add the egg and beat until incorporated.

5. Place an eggplant slice on the work surface. Place 2—3 teaspoons of filling at one end, then gently roll the eggplant lengthwise around the filling. Place in the prepared dish, seam side down. Continue until all the eggplant slices and filling have been used.

6. Pour the remaining sauce over the eggplant rolls and sprinkle with the mozzarella cheese. Place the dish on a baking sheet and bake for 25—30 minutes, until the filling is set and the cheese is golden brown. Let stand for 5 minutes, then serve.

SERVES 4

1 large eggplant, sliced
   lengthwise into 8 slices
2 tablespoons olive oil
½ quantity Simple Marinara
   Sauce (see page 85), or
   2 cups store-bought tomato and
   basil pasta sauce
½ cup ricotta cheese
2 ounces soft goat cheese,
   rind removed, crumbled
¼ cup finely shredded basil
   leaves
finely grated rind of 1 lemon
1 extra-large egg, beaten
1 cup shredded mozzarella cheese
salt and pepper, to taste

Mamá's Tip:
A little freshly grated nutmeg added
to the filling will turn this dish into
a taste sensation!

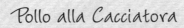

Pollo alla Cacciatora

Chicken Cacciatora

1. Lightly dust the chicken pieces with the flour. Heat the oil in a large skillet. Add the chicken and cook over medium heat until browned all over. Remove from the pan and set aside.

2. Drain off all but 2 tablespoons of the fat in the skillet. Add the wine and simmer, stirring, for a few minutes. Stir in the bell peppers, carrot, celery, and garlic, season with salt and pepper, and simmer for about 15 minutes.

3. Add the browned chicken and tomatoes to the skillet. Cover and simmer, stirring frequently, for 30 minutes, until the chicken is tender and the juices run clear when the tip of a sharp knife is inserted into the thickest part of the meat.

4. Taste and adjust the seasoning, adding salt and pepper, if needed. Transfer to warm bowls, garnish with parsley sprigs, and serve immediately.

SERVES 4

3-pound chicken, cut into
    6 or 8 pieces
1 cup all-purpose flour
3 tablespoons olive oil
⅔ cup dry white wine
1 green bell pepper, seeded and
    sliced
1 red bell pepper, seeded and sliced
1 carrot, finely chopped
1 celery stalk, finely chopped
1 garlic clove, crushed
1 cup canned diced tomatoes
salt and pepper, to taste
fresh flat-leaf parsley sprigs,
    to garnish

Salsiccie & Peperoni
Sausage & Peppers

SERVES 4

¼ cup olive oil
8 Italian sausages
1 large green bell pepper,
    seeded and sliced
1 large red bell pepper, seeded
    and sliced
2 onions, sliced
2 large garlic cloves,
    finely chopped
⅔ cup tomato puree or tomato sauce
salt and pepper, to taste
basil leaves, to garnish

1. Heat the oil in a large skillet with a tight-fitting lid over medium heat. Add the sausages, in batches if necessary, and cook, stirring, until brown all over. Remove from the skillet and set aside. Pour off all but 2 tablespoons of the fat from the skillet.

2. Add the green bell pepper, red bell pepper, and onion to the skillet and cook, stirring, for 3 minutes, until beginning to soften. Add the garlic and stir for an additional 1 minute.

3. Add the tomato puree and season with salt and pepper. Return the sausages to the skillet and bring the mixture to a boil, stirring.

4. Reduce the heat to low, cover, and simmer for 12–15 minutes, until the sausages are cooked through and the bell peppers are tender. Adjust the seasoning, if necessary. Garnish with basil leaves and serve immediately. Alternatively, transfer to a bowl, let cool completely, and serve as a cold appetizer for eight people.

Stufato di Verdure

Italian Vegetable Stew

SERVES 4

4 garlic cloves, minced
1 small acorn squash, diced
1 red onion, sliced
2 leeks, sliced
1 eggplant, sliced
1 small celeriac, diced
2 turnips, sliced
2 plum tomatoes, chopped
1 carrot, sliced
1 zucchini, sliced
2 red bell peppers, seeded and sliced
1 fennel bulb, sliced
6 ounces Swiss chard
2 bay leaves
½ teaspoon fennel seeds
½ teaspoon chili powder
pinch of each dried thyme,
    dried oregano, and sugar
⅔ cup torn fresh basil leaves
½ cup olive oil
1 cup vegetable stock
¼ cup chopped fresh parsley
salt and pepper, to taste
2 tablespoons freshly grated
    Parmesan cheese, to serve

1. Put the garlic and squash in a large, heavy saucepan with all the other vegetables, the bay leaves, fennel seeds, chili powder, thyme, oregano, sugar, and half of the basil.

2. Pour the oil and stock into the saucepan. Mix all the ingredients together well, then bring to a boil.

3. Reduce the heat, cover, and simmer for 30 minutes, or until all the vegetables are tender. Discard the bay leaves.

4. Sprinkle in the remaining basil and the parsley and season with salt and pepper. Serve immediately, sprinkled with the Parmesan.

Filetti di Jacchino
Italian Turkey Cutlets

SERVES 4

1 tablespoon olive oil
4 turkey cutlets
2 red bell peppers, seeded
   and sliced
1 red onion, sliced
2 garlic cloves, finely chopped
1¼ cups tomato puree or
   tomato sauce
⅔ cup medium white wine
1 tablespoon chopped fresh marjoram
1 (15-ounce) can cannellini
   beans, drained and rinsed
¼ cup fresh white bread crumbs
salt and pepper, to taste
fresh basil sprigs, to garnish

1. Heat the oil in a flameproof casserole dish, add the turkey, and cook over medium heat for 5—10 minutes, turning occasionally, until browned all over. Transfer to a plate using a slotted spoon.

2. Add the red bell peppers and onion to the casserole dish and cook over low heat, stirring occasionally, for 5 minutes, or until softened. Add the garlic and cook for an additional 2 minutes.

3. Return the turkey to the casserole dish and add the tomato puree, wine, and marjoram. Season with salt and pepper. Bring to a boil, then reduce the heat, cover, and simmer, stirring occasionally, for 25—30 minutes, or until the turkey is cooked through and the juices run clear when the tip of a sharp knife is inserted into the thickest part of the meat. Meanwhile, preheat the broiler to medium.

4. Stir the cannellini beans into the casserole and simmer for an additional 5 minutes. Sprinkle the bread crumbs over the top and place under the preheated broiler for 2—3 minutes, or until golden. Serve immediately, garnished with basil sprigs.

1. Melt the butter with the oil in a large skillet over medium—high heat. Add the shallots, garlic, and crushed red pepper (if using), and sauté for 1—2 minutes, until the shallots are soft but not brown.

2. Stir in the lemon rind, wine, and lemon juice, bring to a boil, and cook, stirring occasionally, for 2—3 minutes, until the sauce reduces slightly and the flavors blend. If the butter starts to brown, immediately remove the skillet from the heat.

3. Reduce the heat, add the shrimp, and cook, stirring occasionally, for 2—3 minutes, until they turn pink and curl. Stir in the parsley and season with salt and pepper.

4. Meanwhile, bring a large saucepan of lightly salted water to a boil. Add the pasta, bring back to a boil, and cook for 2—4 minutes, or according to the package directions. Drain the pasta well, then immediately add it to the skillet with the shrimp, using two forks to mix and blend all the ingredients together.

5. Divide the pasta and shrimp among warm bowls, pour the cooking juices over the top, and serve immediately.

SERVES 4

1 stick butter
½ cup olive oil
2 shallots, finely chopped
6 garlic cloves, minced
¼ teaspoon crushed red pepper
   (optional)
finely grated rind of
   1 large lemon
⅓ cup dry white wine
2 tablespoons lemon juice
1¼ pounds jumbo shrimp,
   peeled and deveined
2 tablespoons finely chopped
   fresh flat-leaf parsley
12 ounces dried angel hair pasta
salt and pepper, to taste

Mama's Tip:
This recipe is also great with spaghetti,
linguine, or tagliatelle—just use whatever
you have left in the cupboard!

Frittata Primavera
Spring Vegetable Frittata

1. Toast the pine nuts in a large, heavy skillet with a heatproof handle over medium heat, stirring until they are golden brown. Transfer to a plate.

2. Using a fork, lightly beat the eggs in a bowl with the salt and pepper.

3. Preheat the broiler to high. Fill the skillet halfway with water and bring to a boil. Add the asparagus, green beans, and fava beans. Simmer for 2 minutes, then drain.

4. Dry the skillet and return to medium heat. Add the oil and butter and, when melted and foaming, add the vegetables and pour the beaten eggs over the top.

5. Cook the frittata for 1–2 minutes, until lightly browned underneath, then place the skillet under the preheated broiler and cook for 1–2 minutes, until just set in the middle.

6. Pile the Parmesan cheese shavings and arugula on top of the frittata and sprinkle with the pine nuts. Serve immediately with crusty bread.

SERVES 2

2 tablespoons pine nuts
5 eggs
2 ounces fine asparagus
   spears
½ cup green beans
⅓ cup fresh shelled
   baby fava beans or peas
1 teaspoon olive oil
½ tablespoon butter
¼ cup fresh Parmesan
   cheese shavings
handful of arugula leaves
salt and pepper, to taste
crusty bread, to serve

Polenta con Ragù di Funghi
Polenta with Mushroom Ragu

1. To make the ragu, strain the porcini through a strainer lined with cheesecloth or through a coffee filter, then set the liquid aside. Rinse and slice the porcini and set them aside.

2. Heat the oil and butter in a large skillet with a lid over medium heat. Add the wild mushrooms and sauté, stirring, for 5 minutes. Stir in the porcini, garlic, and rosemary and season with salt and pepper. Continue sautéing until the wild mushrooms have released and reabsorbed their liquid.

3. Add the vermouth and ½ cup of the reserved strained liquid and bring to a boil, stirring. Reduce the heat to very low, cover the skillet, and simmer for 15—20 minutes, until the mushrooms are tender and the flavors blend. Adjust the seasoning, if necessary.

SERVES 4

1 (18-ounce) firm polenta log,
   cut into twelve ½-inch slices
garlic-flavored olive oil
chopped fresh flat-leaf
   parsley, to garnish

MUSHROOM RAGU

1 ounce dried porcini, soaked
   in at least ¾ cup hot water
   for at least 30 minutes
3 tablespoons extra virgin
   olive oil
2 tablespoons butter
1¾ pounds mixed wild
   mushrooms, thickly sliced
4 garlic cloves, minced
1 teaspoon dried rosemary
   or thyme
¼ cup red vermouth
salt and pepper, to taste

4. Meanwhile, preheat a ridged grill pan over high heat and preheat the oven to 350°F. Brush the polenta slices with oil, add as many to the pan as will fit in a single layer, and heat for 3 minutes on each side, until marked with black lines and heated through. Transfer the cooked polenta slices to the oven to keep warm while you cook the remainder.

5. Arrange the polenta slices on warm plates and spoon the ragu over them. Garnish with parsley and serve immediately.

Risotto con Polpettine Piccante
Spicy Meatball Risotto

SERVES 4

1 thick slice white bread
water or milk, for soaking
1 pound fresh ground pork
2 garlic cloves, minced
1 tablespoon minced onion
1 teaspoon crushed black
    peppercorns
pinch of salt
1 egg
vegetable oil, for shallow-frying
1 (14½-ounce) can diced tomatoes
1 tablespoon tomato paste
1 teaspoon dried oregano
1 teaspoon fennel seeds
pinch of sugar
1 tablespoon olive oil
3 tablespoons butter
1 small onion, finely chopped
1½ cups risotto rice
⅔ cup red wine
4 cups beef stock
salt and pepper, to taste
fresh basil leaves, to garnish

1. Place the bread into a bowl, add the water, and let soak for 5 minutes. Squeeze out the water and place into a bowl with the pork, garlic, onion, peppercorns, and salt. Add the egg and mix thoroughly. Shape the mixture into 12 equal balls. Heat the vegetable oil in a skillet. Add the meatballs and cook thoroughly. Remove and drain.

2. Combine the tomatoes, paste, herbs, and sugar in a large saucepan. Add the meatballs and bring to a boil. Reduce the heat and simmer for 30 minutes.

3. Heat the oil with 2 tablespoons of butter in a deep saucepan until the butter has melted. Add the onion and cook for 5 minutes, until browned. Reduce the heat, add the rice, and mix to coat. Cook, stirring continuously, for 2—3 minutes, or until the grains are translucent. Add the wine and cook, stirring continuously, until reduced.

4. Gradually add the hot stock. Stir continuously and add more liquid as the rice absorbs each addition. Cook for 20 minutes. Season with salt and pepper. Lift out the cooked meatballs and add to the risotto. Remove the risotto from the heat and add the remaining butter. Mix well. Divide the risotto and meatballs among four warm plates. Drizzle with the tomato sauce, garnish with the basil, and serve immediately.

Pizzaiola
Broiled Steak with Pizzaiola Sauce

SERVES 4

3 tablespoons olive oil,
  plus extra for brushing
6 tomatoes (about 1½ pounds),
  peeled and diced
1 red bell pepper, seeded
  and chopped
1 onion, chopped
2 garlic cloves, minced
1 tablespoon chopped fresh
  flat-leaf parsley
1 teaspoon dried oregano
1 teaspoon sugar
4 tenderloin steaks, about
  6 ounces each
salt and pepper, to taste

1. Place the oil, tomatoes, bell pepper, onion, garlic, parsley, oregano, and sugar in a heavy saucepan and season with salt and pepper. Bring to a boil, lower the heat, and simmer for 15 minutes.

2. Meanwhile, snip any fat around the outsides of the steaks. Season each generously with pepper (no salt) and brush with oil.

3. Preheat the broiler to high. Cook the steaks under the preheated broiler for 1 minute on each side. Lower the heat to medium and cook according to taste: 1½—2 minutes each side for rare; 2½—3 minutes each side for medium; and 3—4 minutes each side for well done.

4. Transfer the steaks to warm individual plates and spoon the sauce over them. Serve immediately.

Scaloppine alla Marsala

Veal Cutlets with Marsala

1. Put each veal cutlet between two pieces of plastic wrap or inside a plastic food bag and, using a rolling pin, gently beat until ⅛ inch thick.

2. Season the cutlets well with salt and pepper and dust with the flour.

3. Heat the oil in a large skillet, add the cutlets, and cook over high heat for 1 minute on each side, or until lightly browned. Add the Marsala and let the liquid simmer around the cutlets for 1 minute.

4. Serve immediately with the juices poured over the meat. Garnish with parsley and serve accompanied by mashed potatoes or a green salad.

SERVES 4

4 veal cutlets, about
   3 ounces each
1 tablespoon all-purpose flour
3 tablespoons olive oil
⅔ cup Marsala
salt and pepper, to taste
handful of chopped fresh
   flat-leaf parsley, to garnish
mashed potatoes or green salad,
   to serve

Mama's Tip:
You can use skinless, boneless chicken
breasts instead of veal—prepare them in
the same way, following the directions
for the veal.

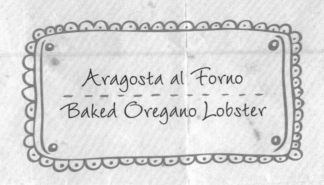

Aragosta al Forno
Baked Oregano Lobster

1. Preheat the oven to 350°F. Bring a saucepan of water to a boil. Select a roasting pan that will hold the lobster tails upright.

2. Put a lobster tail, shell side down, on a cutting board. Use a pair of scissors to cut lengthwise through the shell without cutting through the tail fan and being careful not to crush the shell. Use a small knife to cut the tail meat in half lengthwise without cutting through the shell. Use the scissors to cut away the tough cartilage on top of the shell. Use the tip of a knife to cut out the black intestinal vein and remove. Repeat with the remaining tails. Cover and refrigerate the tails until required.

3. Heat the oil in a skillet. Add the shallot and sauté for 1—2 minutes, until lightly brown. Add the garlic and stir for an additional 1 minute, or until the shallot is soft. Stir in the bread crumbs, oregano, lemon rind, and parsley and season with salt and pepper.

4. Lightly season inside the split tails, then place them in the roasting pan, using balls of aluminum foil to wedge them upright, if necessary. Divide the oregano mixture among the four tails, lightly pressing it into the splits, but not packing it in, and covering half the tails. You might have a little left over, depending on the size of the tails. Drizzle with oil.

5. Add enough boiling water to the pan to come halfway up the sides of the tails, being careful not to get any water on the stuffing. Bake in the preheated oven for 20 minutes, until the flesh at the thickest part under the stuffing is white. Remove from the oven and serve immediately.

SERVES 4

4 frozen lobster tails, about
  6 ounces each, thawed and
  patted dry
¼ cup olive oil, plus extra
  for drizzling
1 large shallot, minced
2 garlic cloves, minced
⅓ cup fine dry bread crumbs
2 teaspoons dried oregano
finely grated rind of 2 lemons
1 tablespoon finely chopped
  fresh flat-leaf parsley
salt and pepper, to taste

Tonno Condito
Marinated Tuna Steaks

1. To make the marinade, combine the oil, orange juice, ripe black olives, green olives, tomatoes, roasted red pepper, thyme, and orange rind in a nonmetallic bowl. Season with salt and pepper and set aside.

2. Heat a large, ridged grill pan over medium—high heat until a splash of water "dances" on the surface. Brush one side of each tuna steak with oil, place it in the pan, and season the top with salt and pepper. Cook for 2 minutes, then turn and cook on the other side for an additional 2 minutes for rare, or up to 5 minutes for well done.

3. Transfer the tuna steaks to a deep serving dish that will hold them all in a single layer. Pour the marinade over the top of the tuna steaks and set aside to cool.

SERVES 4

4 tuna steaks, about
 5 ounces each
2 tablespoons olive oil
1 fennel bulb, thinly sliced
salt and pepper, to taste
arugula and crusty bread,
 to serve

MARINADE
½ cup olive oil
2 tablespoons orange juice
½ cup each diced, pitted ripe
 black olives and green olives
2 large tomatoes, peeled,
 seeded, and diced
1 large roasted red pepper,
 seeded and sliced
leaves from 4 fresh thyme
 sprigs, or 2 teaspoons
 dried thyme
finely grated rind of 1 orange
salt and pepper, to taste

4. Meanwhile, brush the fennel slices with oil, then place them in the pan in a single layer and heat until lightly marked with lines on both sides. Transfer to the bowl with the tuna, pushing them down into the marinade.

5. To serve, place the tuna steaks on plates and spoon the fennel, olives, and tomatoes over, then add the marinade sauce. Top with the arugula leaves. Serve with plenty of bread for mopping up the delicious marinade sauce.

Saltimbocca
Pork Rolls

SERVES 4

4 pork chops, bones and
   fat removed
4 large, thin slices
   proscuitto
4 large sage leaves
1 stick unsalted butter
1 cup Marsala, Madeira,
   or dry white wine
salt and pepper, to taste
sautéed potatoes and a green
   salad, to serve

1. Lay the pork chops on a board and flatten them with a meat mallet or rolling pin until they are the same size as the prosciutto slices. Lay down a piece of prosciutto, put a piece of pork on top, and place a sage leaf at the edge nearest to you.

2. Season with salt and pepper, then roll the meat around the sage leaf and secure it with a toothpick. The prosciutto should be on the outside. Repeat with all four chops.

3. Place a wide, heavy saucepan over high heat. Add the butter and then the meat rolls and brown them quickly on all sides. Add the Marsala and reduce the heat to a simmer.

4. Cover and cook for about 10—15 minutes, until the meat is cooked through. The pork should not show any pink traces and the juices should run clear when pierced with a the tip of a sharp knife.

5. Remove the rolls with a slotted spoon and keep them warm. Increase the heat and reduce the liquid for 2 minutes to thicken. Serve the rolls immediately with sautéed potatoes and a green salad and pour a little of the sauce over them.

A good family get-together can involve people from three or four generations. When Mama has all her *bambini* home, my table will cater for old-timers like me and Alberto to my *pronipoti*, my beautiful great grandchildren.

A big family is a gift from heaven — but taking care of guests of all ages means a little planning might be needed.

Always include the *bambini*. In Apulia, we say "Nelle botti piccine ci sta il vino buono," or "in the small barrels you find the good wine." Why do some people insist on the little ones eating separately? With children at the table, there is always more joy.

Try to seat people where everyone can see everyone else — but keep parents near their *bambini*. The old like to see the energy of the young — but they may not be so quick to deal with an unruly child.

At Casa di Mama, everyone earns their dinner! Some help me in the kitchen, some choose the vino with Alberto. Others tell stories, sing songs, or play games with the little ones. There should be no silence, no formality! This is a family dinner, remember, not having an audience with Il Papa at the Vatican!

120

Celebrate the fact that you are all together—share in the wisdom of the old and the vigor of the young.

There is an Italian proverb: "Chi mangia solo, crepa solo" — he who eats alone, dies alone. The best food tastes better in company; don't save your big gatherings for special occasions. Being alive and with people you love is cause enough for celebration.

Have something planned for after you have eaten. Games for the children, quieter time for the older guests. We all digest at our own pace.

Filetti di Salmone con Pesto
Salmon Fillets with Pesto

SERVES 4

4 salmon steaks, about
   6 ounces each
mixed salad and toasted
   ciabatta, to serve

PARSLEY PESTO
2 garlic cloves, coarsely chopped
¼ cup pine nuts
¾ cup fresh flat-leaf parsley,
   coarse stems removed
1 teaspoon salt
¼ cup freshly grated
   Parmesan cheese
½ cup extra virgin olive oil,
   plus extra if needed

1. To make the parsley pesto, put the garlic, pine nuts, parsley, and salt into a food processor or blender and process to a puree.

2. Add the Parmesan and blend briefly again. Then add the olive oil and blend again. If the consistency is too thick, add some extra oil and blend again until smooth. Scrape into a bowl and set aside.

3. Meanwhile, preheat the broiler to medium. Cook the salmon under the preheated broiler for 10—15 minutes, depending on the thickness of the fish, until the flesh turns pink and flakes easily.

4. Transfer the salmon to serving plates, top with the parsley pesto, and serve immediately with salad and ciabatta.

bianco

Ribollita
Italian Cabbage & Bean Stew

1. Heat the olive oil in a large saucepan and cook the onions, carrots, and celery over medium heat, stirring frequently, for 10—15 minutes. Add the garlic, thyme, and season with salt and pepper. Continue to cook for an additional 1—2 minutes, until the vegetables are golden.

2. Add the cannellini beans to the pan and pour in the tomatoes. Add enough of the water to cover the vegetables.

3. Bring to a boil, then reduce the heat and simmer for 20 minutes. Add the parsley and cabbage and cook for an additional 5 minutes.

4. Stir in the bread and add a little more water, if necessary. The consistency should be thick.

5. Taste and adjust the seasoning, adding salt and pepper, if necessary. Serve immediately, drizzled with extra virgin olive oil.

SERVES 4

3 tablespoons olive oil
2 red onions, coarsely chopped
3 carrots, sliced
3 celery stalks, coarsely chopped
3 garlic cloves, chopped
1 tablespoon chopped fresh thyme
1 (15-ounce) can cannellini beans, drained and rinsed
1 (14-ounce) can diced tomatoes
about 2½ cups water or vegetable stock
2 tablespoons chopped fresh parsley
1 small head savoy cabbage or green cabbage, cored and sliced
1 small day-old ciabatta loaf, torn into pieces
salt and pepper, to taste
extra virgin olive oil, to serve

Superbo Sides & Salads

Do you want to know what marks out the maestro from the rest of the crowd? What elevates the artist to genius? *Attenzione ai dettagli* — attention to detail. Sure, you can have your steaks, your stews, your cutlets — but man cannot live on meat alone! And Mama cannot feed a family with meals lacking the vegetable side dishes, the salads, and all the *attenzione ai dettagli* that keep them coming back for more every day. Don't neglect your sides or salads! Doing so is the mark of the amateur cook! And, if they are properly done with the freshest vegetables, the crispiest greens, or the sweetest herbs, a good Spinach in Gorgonzola, Carpaccio Salad, or even Mama-Style Roasted Potatoes can be as beautiful a thing as you will see on any Italian family dinner table!

Peperoni & Cipolle

Slow-Cooked Peppers & Onions

SERVES 4

3 tablespoons olive oil
1 large onion, thinly sliced
3 mixed bell peppers, such as red, orange, and yellow, seeded and cut into strips
2 garlic cloves, finely chopped
1 (14½-ounce) can diced tomatoes
2 teaspoons dried thyme
salt and pepper, to taste

1. Heat the oil in a large skillet with a tight-fitting lid over medium heat. Stir in the onion, cover, reduce the heat to low, and simmer for 8—10 minutes, until the onion is soft but not brown.

2. Stir in the mixed bell peppers and garlic and season with salt and pepper. Replace the lid and simmer for 5 minutes.

3. Stir in the tomatoes and thyme and bring to a boil, stirring. Reduce the heat to low (use a heat diffuser if you have one), replace the lid, and let simmer for 20 minutes, until the bell peppers are tender. If the sauce is too runny, uncover and boil until it reaches the desired consistency. Adjust the seasoning, if necessary.

4. Spoon into a serving dish and serve hot or at room temperature.

Cime di Rapa Gratinate
Broccoli Rabe Gratin

1. To make the sauce, put the milk, bay leaves, and onion into a small saucepan with a pinch of salt and bring to simmering point. Remove from the heat, cover, and let stand for at least 1 hour for the flavors to blend. Strain the milk and set aside.

2. Melt the butter in a saucepan over medium—high heat. Add the flour and stir for 2 minutes, until it is blended and a paste forms. Remove the pan from the heat and gradually add the milk, stirring continuously, until it is blended and the sauce is smooth. Return to the heat and bring to just below boiling point, then reduce the heat and simmer for 5 minutes. Season with salt and pepper and set aside.

3. Meanwhile, preheat the broiler to high and position the broiler rack about 2 inches below the heat. Bring a large saucepan of lightly salted water to a boil.

SERVES 4

1¾ bunches of broccoli rabe
  (rapini; about 1¾ pounds)
⅓ cup freshly grated
  Parmesan cheese
salt and pepper, to taste

WHITE SAUCE
1¼ cups milk
2 bay leaves
½ onion, studded with 4 cloves
2 tablespoons butter, plus
  extra for greasing
2 tablespoons Italian 00 flour
  or all-purpose flour
salt and pepper, to taste

4. Remove and discard the thick ends of the broccoli rabe stems and any yellow leaves. Separate the thin stems with leaves from the thick stems with flower heads. Rinse the broccoli well in several changes of cold water.

5. Add the thick stems with flower heads to the boiling water and boil for 2 minutes. Then add the thin stems and boil for 6—8 minutes, until all the stems are tender. Drain well, squeezing out any excess moisture.

6. Grease a shallow baking dish. Spread the broccoli rabe over the bottom of the dish and season with salt and pepper. Pour the sauce over the vegetable and sprinkle with the cheese.

7. Place the dish under the preheated broiler and cook for 10—12 minutes, until the top is bubbling and golden. Let stand for 2 minutes, then serve.

Spinaci in Gorgonzola
Spinach in Gorgonzola Sauce

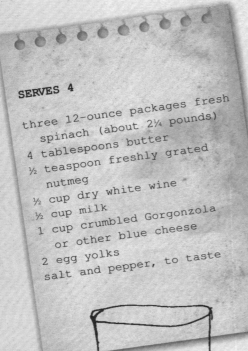

SERVES 4

three 12-ounce packages fresh
  spinach (about 2¼ pounds)
4 tablespoons butter
½ teaspoon freshly grated
  nutmeg
½ cup dry white wine
½ cup milk
1 cup crumbled Gorgonzola
  or other blue cheese
2 egg yolks
salt and pepper, to taste

Bianco

1. Remove and discard any tough stems from the spinach, then place the leaves in a colander and wash under cold running water. Let drain.

2. Melt half of the butter in a large saucepan over medium heat. Stir in the spinach, with the water still clinging to its leaves, cover, and cook for 3—4 minutes, until wilted.

3. Stir in the nutmeg and season with salt and pepper, then reduce the heat to low to keep the spinach warm while you prepare the sauce.

4. Pour the wine and milk into a separate saucepan, bring to a boil, then simmer until reduced slightly. Add the Gorgonzola and stir until melted. Remove from the heat.

5. Beat the egg yolks in a small bowl, stir in a little of the hot sauce, then transfer to the pan with the remaining butter and the spinach. Stir thoroughly and place over medium heat until warm.

6. Taste and adjust the seasoning, adding salt and pepper if necessary. Serve immediately.

Mama's guide to growing vegetables

They say that man cannot live on bread alone (not even Mama's superbo focaccia!) — but it is also true that meat by itself cannot make a meal. Italian cooking is rooted in the land — and that means knowing how to make the best of what nature provides. My verdura — my vegetables — are Mama's great secret. From the crispiest salade to the sweetest zucchini, these are what elevate simple dinners to grande arte!

And best of all? You can grow them yourself. Nothing — and I mean niente — tastes better than homegrown vegetables, picked and prepared and served within minutes. Here are Mama's tips for growing three of the best for yourself.

Artichokes

These wonderful plants make beautiful flowers as well as tasting sublime with butter. They can be difficult to grow from seeds, so buy as little, *poco* plants and plant them into a sunny spot in your yard in fall. Feed with a monthly side dressing of compost.

In the first year, it is *importante* to remove flower heads — this will help the plant grow strong. After that, the flowers can be lopped off and eaten as they form in the summer. *Delizioso!*

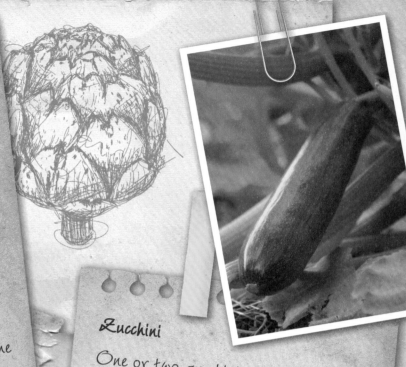

Eggplants

These can be grown on a windowsill if your yard is small or you live in the city — and will provide a hint of Apulia on even a gray day. Choose seeds for a dwarf, busy eggplant. Sow a couple of seeds into a flowerpot in early spring, place a clear plastic bag on top, and put on a sunny windowsill. When the shoots appear, remove the bag, and as the plant gets bigger, replant in a bigger flowerpot. As they get bigger, support them with a stake.

Zucchini

One or two zucchini plants in your vegetable garden will keep producing all summer long. Plant as seeds into small flowerpots two weeks before the last expected frost date and then transplant to a sunny, sheltered spot when the soil temperature reaches 60°F. Give them plenty of room — they can grow *molto grande!*

Keep well watered and pick the zucchini as they appear — the more you harvest, the more they are encouraged to grow! I like them at 4 inches long.

Carciofi alla Romana
Roman-Style Artichokes

SERVES 4

1 tablespoon lemon juice
4 globe artichokes
⅓ cup finely chopped fresh
   flat-leaf parsley
leaves from 8 fresh mint
   sprigs, finely chopped
4 large garlic cloves,
   2 minced, 2 sliced
1 cup olive oil
1¼ cups dry white wine
salt and pepper, to taste

1. Preheat the oven to 325°F. Put the lemon juice in a bowl of cold water large enough to hold the artichokes and set aside.

2. To prepare the artichokes, remove all the outer leaves and trim the stems. Cut off the top of each artichoke and remove and discard the hairy choke. Drop each artichoke in the bowl of lemon water to prevent discoloration.

3. Mix together the parsley, mint, minced garlic, and 3 tablespoons of the oil and season well. Remove the artichokes from the water and drain on paper towels.

4. Divide the mint mixture among the artichokes, pressing the filling into each hole left by the chokes. Transfer the artichokes to a deep baking dish that will hold the artichokes upright. Mix together the remaining oil and the wine and pour around the artichokes. Sprinkle with the sliced garlic and cover with aluminum foil. Bake in the preheated oven for 40—50 minutes, until the artichokes are tender. Remove the artichokes from the dish and let cool.

5. Transfer the cooking liquid to a small saucepan and boil until reduced by half. Remove the garlic slices, adjust the seasoning, and set aside to cool. When both the juices and artichokes are cool, return the artichokes to the sauce, standing upright, and chill in the refrigerator for up to two days. Remove the artichokes from the refrigerator 15 minutes before serving to bring to room temperature. Serve with the juices spooned over the artichokes.

Scafata
Umbrian-Style Fava Beans

SERVES 4

3 tablespoons olive oil
1 carrot, finely chopped
1 celery stalk, finely chopped
½ onion, finely chopped
4 large tomatoes
2½ cups shelled fava beans,
    thawed if frozen
⅔ cup tomato puree or
    tomato sauce
2 tablespoons water
4 fresh thyme sprigs
2 bay leaves
pinch of sugar
salt and pepper, to taste
extra virgin olive oil,
    to serve (optional)

1. Heat the olive oil in a saucepan over high heat. Add the carrot, celery, and onion and reduce the heat to low. Cover the pan and simmer for 8—10 minutes, or until the onion is soft but not brown.

2. Meanwhile, bring a saucepan of lightly salted water to a boil. Cut an "X" in the stem end of the tomatoes, add them to the pan of water, and blanch for 2—3 minutes, until the skins split. Drain and place under cold running water. Peel and seed the tomatoes, then chop the flesh.

3. Stir the beans, tomatoes, tomato puree, water, thyme, bay leaves, and sugar into the onion mixture. Season with salt and pepper and bring to a boil. Reduce the heat to low, cover, and simmer for 30—40 minutes, until the beans and other vegetables are tender.

4. Remove the thyme sprigs and bay leaves and adjust the seasoning, if necessary. Spoon into a serving bowl and serve with extra virgin olive oil on the side (if using).

Cicoria con Aglio
Escarole with Garlic

1. Heat the oil in a large skillet over medium heat.

2. Add the garlic and stir for 2 minutes, or until fragrant. Be careful that the garlic does not burn or overcook.

3. Add the escarole and stir until it is well coated in the oil. Increase the heat to high and continue to stir for 3—5 minutes, or until wilted and tender.

4. Stir in the lemon juice and season with salt and pepper. Serve immediately.

Mama's Tip:
The flavor of escarole can be a little bitter for some tastes so, if you prefer, try using baby spinach instead.

SERVES 4

¼ cup olive oil
4 garlic cloves, thinly sliced
1 pound escarole, frisée, or radicchio, rinsed, torn into bite-size pieces, and shaken dry
freshly squeezed lemon juice, to taste
salt and pepper, to taste

SERVES 4

4 fresh rosemary sprigs
5 russet or Yukon gold
   potatoes, cut into
   small pieces
small handful of fresh
   basil leaves
½ cup extra virgin olive oil,
   plus extra to taste
salt and pepper, to taste

1. Place the rosemary in a large saucepan of lightly salted water and bring to a boil. Bring a smaller saucepan of unsalted water to a boil. Set aside a small bowl of iced water.

2. Add the potatoes to the salted water, bring back to a boil, and cook, partly covered, for 20–25 minutes, until tender but not falling apart. Remove from the heat and let cool without draining.

3. Meanwhile, drop the basil leaves into the unsalted water, push them down with a wooden spoon, and boil for just a few seconds, until they wilt. Drain and place in the iced water to cool. Remove and pat completely dry with paper towels, then finely chop and set aside.

4. Drain the cooled potatoes and rosemary, reserving about ¼ cup of the cooking water and the rosemary. Return the potatoes to the pan with the reserved water and season with salt and pepper. Break them up using an electric handheld mixer.

5. When they begin to mash, slowly beat in the oil, then stir in the reserved rosemary and the basil. Adjust the seasoning, if necessary, and serve immediately.

Patate al Forno

Italian Herb Roasted Potatoes

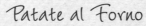

SERVES 4

3 fresh rosemary sprigs, plus
    extra to garnish
14 small potatoes (about 1¼ pounds),
    cubed
3 garlic cloves, coarsely chopped
⅓ cup olive oil, plus extra
    for oiling
salt and pepper, to taste

1. Preheat the oven to 400°F. Brush a large baking dish with oil.

2. Remove the leaves from the rosemary sprigs, discarding the stems, and chop the leaves coarsely. Set aside.

3. Place a layer of potatoes in the prepared baking dish, then sprinkle with a little of the garlic and rosemary and season with salt and pepper. Repeat the layers until all the potatoes, garlic, and rosemary have been used.

4. Drizzle with the olive oil, then transfer the dish to the preheated oven and cook, stirring frequently, for 45 minutes, or until the potatoes are tender and lightly browned.

5. Garnish with a rosemary sprig and serve the potatoes immediately, straight from the baking dish.

Mama's Tip:
Use some finely chopped fresh mint instead of the rosemary for a fresh-tasting alternative.

Frittate di Formaggio e Patate
Mini Cheese & Potato Frittatas

1. Bring a saucepan of lightly salted water to a boil. Add the potatoes, bring back to a boil, and cook for 12—15 minutes, until tender. Drain well and cool under cold running water.

2. Meanwhile, preheat the oven to 375°F. Generously grease a 12-cup muffin pan. When the potatoes are cool enough to handle, peel and finely chop them, then squeeze out the excess moisture.

3. Beat together the eggs and milk in a bowl. Stir in the potatoes, roasted red peppers, two-thirds of the cheese, and all of the chives. Season with salt and pepper.

4. Divide the mixture equally among the cups in the prepared muffin pan, filling each just under halfway full. Sprinkle the remaining cheese over the tops of the frittatas, being careful not to get it on the edge of the frittatas.

5. Place the pan in the preheated oven and bake for 25—30 minutes, until the frittatas are set and golden brown.

6. Remove the pan from the oven and run a blunt knife around each one, then tip them out. Transfer to a platter and either serve immediately or let cool to room temperature.

MAKES 12

3-4 new potatoes (about 4 ounces),
  unpeeled and scrubbed
olive oil or sunflower oil,
  for greasing
4 eggs
½ cup milk
2 roasted red peppers in oil,
  drained and finely chopped
1 cup grated Parmesan cheese
  or pecorino cheese
2 tablespoons finely snipped
  chives
salt and pepper, to taste

Mama's Tip:
You can substitute three finely chopped
slices of prosciutto for the roasted
red peppers.

143

Insalata di Cesare
Caesar Salad

SERVES 4

½ cup olive oil
2 garlic cloves
5 slices white bread, crusts removed, cut into ½-inch cubes
1 egg
3 Boston lettuces
2 tablespoons lemon juice
8 canned anchovy fillets, drained and coarsely chopped
salt and pepper, to taste
fresh Parmesan cheese shavings, to serve

1. Heat ¼ cup of the oil in a heavy skillet. Add the garlic and bread and cook, stirring frequently, for 4—5 minutes, until the bread is crisp and golden.

2. Remove the croutons from the skillet with a slotted spoon and drain on paper towels. Discard the garlic.

3. Meanwhile, bring a small saucepan of water to a boil. Add the egg and cook for 1 minute, then remove from the pan and set aside.

4. Break apart the lettuce and arrange the leaves in a bowl. In a separate bowl, add the remaining oil and the lemon juice, season with salt and pepper, and mix.

5. Crack the egg into the lemon dressing and whisk to blend. Pour the dressing over the lettuce and toss well.

6. Add the chopped anchovies and croutons. Toss the salad again. Sprinkle with Parmesan cheese shavings and serve immediately.

Carpaccio
Carpaccio Salad

1. To make the mayonnaise, finely chop the anchovy fillets on a cutting board, use the tip of a knife to mash them into a paste, then set aside. Put the egg yolk, half of the lemon juice, and pepper into a bowl. Beat with an electric handheld mixer or a hand whisk. Begin to add the olive oil drop by drop, beating continuously, until the mixture thickens.

2. Beat in the reserved oil from the anchovies, then slowly add the remaining olive oil in a slow, steady stream until the mixture thickens. Beat in the anchovies. Taste and add the remaining lemon juice, if desired, and season with salt and pepper. Slowly stir in a boiling water until the mayonnaise is thin enough to just flow off the tip of a spoon. Transfer to a bowl, cover, and chill until required. (Leftover mayonnaise can be stored in the refrigerator for up to three days.)

SERVES 4

9–12 ounces tenderloin steak,
  sliced wafer thin
2 tablespoons tiny capers,
  rinsed and dried
1 tablespoon minced shallot
salt and pepper, to taste
finely chopped fresh flat-leaf
  parsley, to garnish

ANCHOVY MAYONNAISE

6 anchovy fillets in oil,
  drained, 1 teaspoon of the
  oil reserved
1 egg yolk, at room
  temperature
1 teaspoon lemon juice
½ cup extra virgin olive oil
½–2 tablespoons boiling water,
  plus extra if needed
salt and pepper, to taste

3. Arrange the steak on a platter. Sprinkle with the capers and shallot and season with salt and pepper, keeping in mind that the capers are salty.

4. Stir the mayonnaise and thin it with a little extra boiling water, if it has thickened. Drizzle the mayonnaise over the carpaccio, garnish with parsley, and serve.

Mama's Tip:
The best way to get wafer-thin slices of beef is to ask a butcher to do it for you. If you slice it yourself, buy the larger quantity of steak. Place in the freezer for 20 minutes, then use a thin, sharp knife. Layer the pieces of steak between sheets of plastic wrap and transfer them directly to the platter, without overlapping.

Insalata di Rucola & Parmigiana

Arugula & Parmesan Salad

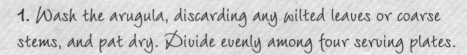

SERVES 4

2 handfuls of arugula leaves
1 small fennel bulb
⅓ cup olive oil
2 tablespoons balsamic vinegar
⅓ cup pine nuts
1 cup Parmesan cheese shavings
salt and pepper, to taste

1. Wash the arugula, discarding any wilted leaves or coarse stems, and pat dry. Divide evenly among four serving plates.

2. Halve the fennel bulb and slice it finely. Arrange the sliced fennel over the arugula.

3. Whisk together the oil and balsamic vinegar with salt and pepper. Drizzle a little of the dressing over each serving.

4. Toast the pine nuts in a dry skillet over high heat until golden brown.

5. Top the salad with the Parmesan shavings and the toasted pine nuts. Serve immediately.

Insalata Rustica
- - - - - - - - - - - -
Country-Style Salad

1. Bring two saucepans of lightly salted water to a boil. Add the potatoes to one pan, bring back to a boil, and cook for 20—25 minutes, until tender. Add the cauliflower florets to the other pan, bring back to a boil, and cook for 5 minutes, or until tender-crisp.

2. Meanwhile, whisk together the oil, vinegar, and salt and pepper in a serving bowl.

3. Use a slotted spoon to remove the cauliflower florets from the pan, shaking off the excess water, and stir them into the dressing in the bowl.

4. Drop the beans into the cauliflower cooking water, bring back to a boil, and cook for 5 minutes, or until tender-crisp. Drain well, then stir into the serving bowl.

5. Drain the potatoes and cool slightly under cold running water. Peel and cut into bite-size pieces, then stir into the dressing along with the scallions and radish. Make sure all the vegetables are coated with dressing, then set aside for at least 1 hour.

6. When ready to serve, line a platter with radicchio leaves. Stir the spinach into the serving bowl and add extra oil, vinegar, and salt and pepper, if desired. Stir in the pine nuts and raisins.

7. Spoon the salad onto the radicchio leaves, adding any dressing left in the bowl. Serve with plenty of ciabatta bread to mop up the dressing.

SERVES 4

5–7 new potatoes (about 10 ounces)
1½ cups small cauliflower florets
¼ cup extra virgin olive oil,
   plus extra if needed
1½ tablespoons red wine vinegar,
   plus extra if needed
2 cups green bean pieces
4 scallions, finely chopped
1 radish, thinly sliced
3 cups baby spinach leaves
2 tablespoons toasted pine nuts
2 tablespoons raisins or
   golden raisins
salt and pepper, to taste
radicchio leaves and ciabatta
   bread, to serve

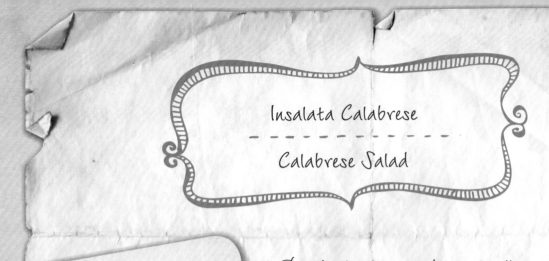

Insalata Calabrese

Calabrese Salad

SERVES 4

8 ounces buffalo mozzarella
  cheese, thinly sliced
2 large beefsteak tomatoes,
  cut into ¼-inch slices
6 large fresh basil leaves
sea salt and pepper, to taste
extra virgin olive oil and aged
  balsamic vinegar, to serve

1. Divide the cheese and tomato slices among four plates, arranging them decoratively in a circular wheel shape. Sprinkle with salt and pepper.

2. Lay the basil leaves on top of each other, roll up in a log shape, and thinly slice crosswise to make fine shreds.

3. Sprinkle the basil shreds over the salads and serve immediately, with oil and vinegar drizzled over the top. Place the olive oil and the vinegar on the table so that more can be added, if desired.

Mama's Tip:
In winter, when tomatoes are pale and flavorless, this simple salad is better made with sun-dried tomatoes and with snipped chives replacing the basil.

1. Preheat the broiler to medium—high and position the broiler rack about 3 inches below the heat. Brush the chicken thighs with oil and season with salt and pepper. Brush the rack with a little oil, add the chicken thighs, skin side up, and cook for 20—25 minutes, or until the chicken is cooked through and the juices run clear when the tip of a sharp knife is inserted into the thickest part of the meat. Remove from the heat and set aside.

2. Meanwhile, bring a large saucepan of lightly salted water to a boil. Add the pasta, return to a boil, and cook according to the package directions, until tender but still firm to the bite. Add the beans 5 minutes before the end of the cooking time.

3. Drain the pasta and beans well and immediately transfer into a large bowl. Add the pesto and stir until the pasta and beans are well coated. Set aside to cool.

4. When the chicken is cool enough to handle, remove the skin and bones and cut the flesh into bite—size pieces. Stir into the pesto mixture and season with salt and pepper. Set aside to cool completely, then cover and refrigerate for up to a day, until required.

5. Remove the salad from the refrigerator 10 minutes before serving. Arrange the tomato slices on a serving platter. Stir the salad and add extra pesto, if needed. Mound the salad on top of the tomatoes, garnish with basil leaves, and serve immediately.

SERVES 4

4 large chicken thighs
sunflower oil or olive oil,
    for brushing
8 ounces dried fusilli
    (corkscrew) pasta
2 cups chopped green beans
1 cup store-bought pesto,
    plus extra if needed
2 large tomatoes, sliced
salt and pepper, to taste
fresh basil leaves, to garnish

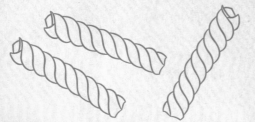

Magnifico Holiday Meals

Holidays! These are the most magical times for a mother (and a grandmother — and especially a great grandmother!). It is during the holidays when all the little chicks come home to Mama's coop. It's a time for the best wines, the tastiest food, and for laughter and love. It is a time for families — and for the family cook, it is a time to show the very best of what you can do in the kitchen. If the simplest way I can express my daily love for my family is by putting my heart and soul into every meal I set down before them, then it is during the holidays that I can elevate that love into something *molto speciale*. At Christmas, Easter, New Year's Eve, and all the other Carnivales that light up the year like stars across the skies — these are the times when Mama shows just what she has become so loved for, by providing a lovely array of comfort food and sweet treats.

Mama's guide to an Italian Christmas

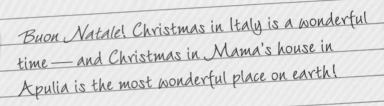

Buon Natale! Christmas in Italy is a wonderful time — and Christmas in Mama's house in Apulia is the most wonderful place on earth!

Christmas is all about *famiglia* — and Mama is lucky enough to always have the *bambini* around at this time of year — my children, and my children's children, and even their children, my *pronipoti*, will all come together every year to eat, drink, laugh, give thanks, and celebrate the season.

In Italy, we have many traditions unique to our country. Our *bambini*, for instance, don't write letters to Santa Claus asking for the latest electronic gadgets — they write letters to their parents, telling them why they love them.

But of course, in Mama's house, when we come together at Christmas, we come together most often around the dinner table. Not just for Christmas dinner (although Mama's Rolled Stuffed Turkey Breast is an unmissable part of the season!), but for many meals throughout the festive period.

Christmas cooking is not just about *uno grosso* meal — it's about what you cook over the whole season. Clams with Spaghetti or Baked Fish are traditional Christmas Eve dinners. Baked Eggplant is our usual dish to eat on Christmas morning (we often go to morning Mass and this stops our stomachs from rumbling during the service).

And then, of course, there are all the sweet things — Mama feels no guilt about indulging everyone at this time of year: Panforte, Panettone, Chocolate & Pear Cake, Struffoli, Ricciarelli — all of these treats are simple to make, delicious to eat, and add to the joy of Christmas at *Casa di Mama!*

Petto di Tacchino Farcito
- - - - - - - - - - - - - - -
Rolled Stuffed
Turkey Breast

1. Preheat the oven to 375°F. Open out the turkey and cover it with a sheet of plastic wrap. Use a meat mallet or rolling pin to pound it into a rectangle no more than ½ inch thick. Season with salt and pepper and cover with the prosciutto slices, then set aside.

2. To make the stuffing, heat the oil in a large skillet over medium heat. Add the sausage meat and cook, stirring to break it up, for 3—5 minutes, until brown and cooked through. Use a slotted spoon to remove the meat, leaving 1 tablespoon of oil in the skillet.

3. Add the shallot to the skillet and sauté, stirring, for 1—2 minutes, until starting to brown. Stir in the garlic and crushed red pepper (if using), and stir for an additional minute. Add the bread crumbs and season with salt and pepper. Stir in the parsley.

4. Place the turkey breast, skin side down, on a work surface. Make a cut along the length of the breast, down the center, without cutting all the way through. Mound the stuffing into the center, then spread it over the top of the breast, leaving a ½-inch border all around. Arrange the roasted pepper slices on top of the stuffing. Roll up the turkey in a jelly-roll fashion. Use kitchen string to tie it in three or four places.

5. Add the oil to the skillet and heat over high heat. Add the turkey and cook for 3—5 minutes, or until golden brown. Transfer to a roasting pan and roast in the preheated oven for 35—40 minutes, or until the juices run clear when cut into with a sharp knife. Transfer to a cutting board, cover with aluminum foil, and let rest for 8—10 minutes before slicing and serving.

SERVES 4–6

3½ pound boneless turkey
  breast, butterflied
4–6 slices prosciutto
1 tablespoon olive oil
salt and pepper, to taste

SAUSAGE & PEPPER STUFFING
1 tablespoon olive oil,
  plus extra if needed
8 ounces spicy Italian sausages,
  casings removed, meat crumbled
1 shallot, finely chopped
2 garlic cloves, chopped
¼ teaspoon crushed red pepper
  (optional)
1 cup fine dry bread crumbs
2 tablespoons finely chopped fresh
  flat-leaf parsley
2 roasted red peppers in olive
  oil, drained and sliced
salt and pepper, to taste

Pesce al Forno
Baked Fish

1. Preheat the oven to 425°F and grease a roasting dish large enough to hold the fish and potatoes.

2. Arrange the potatoes, garlic, and onions in a layer on the bottom of the dish, drizzle with half of the oil, and season with salt and pepper. Tightly cover the dish with aluminum foil and bake in the preheated oven for 30 minutes, until the potatoes are almost tender.

3. Meanwhile, make three slashes on each side of the fish and rub salt and pepper into the slashes. Divide the thyme sprigs and lemon slices among the fish slashes, then set aside.

4. Reduce the oven temperature to 375°F. Uncover the dish and stir the olives into the potatoes. Arrange the fish on top, drizzle with the remaining oil, return to the oven, and cook for 10 minutes per 1 inch of fish thickness, or until the fish is cooked through and the flesh flakes easily.

5. Remove the dish from the oven. Fillet and skin the fish and divide the fillets among four warm plates. Serve with the potatoes, onions, and olives, along with lemon wedges for squeezing over the fish.

Mama's Tip:
This dish was invented for Christmas Eve in Italy, where people go to Midnight Mass and don't want to eat a heavy meal beforehand. It can be adapted to serve a larger number by increasing the ingredients and using a second roasting dish.

SERVES 4

9-12 firm, new potatoes (about
 1 pound), thinly sliced
1 large garlic clove, minced
2 onions, thinly sliced
2 tablespoons olive oil, plus
 extra for greasing
2 (6-7-ounce) whole sea bass,
 red snapper,or Alaskan
 pollock, heads removed,
 scaled, gutted, and well
 rinsed
4 fresh thyme sprigs
½ lemon, sliced
1½ cups sliced, pitted ripe
 black olives
salt and pepper, to taste
lemon wedges, to serve

Spaghetti alle Vongole
Clams with Spaghetti

SERVES 4

2¼ pounds small clams, scrubbed
12 ounces dried spaghetti
½ cup olive oil
4 garlic cloves, chopped
½ cup dry white wine
¼ cup chopped fresh flat-leaf parsley
salt and pepper, to taste

1. Discard any clams with broken shells and any that refuse to close when tapped, then set the remainder aside.

2. Bring a large saucepan of heavily salted water to a boil. Add the spaghetti and boil for 2 minutes less than specified in the package directions. Set the pasta aside, keeping it in the cooking water.

3. Meanwhile, heat the oil in a large, deep skillet over medium heat. Add the garlic and stir for a minute, until golden but not brown.

4. Increase the heat to high, add the wine, and let simmer for 2 minutes, or until reduced by half. Add the clams and stir for 2–3 minutes, until they open. Discard any clams that remain closed.

5. Add 1 cup of the pasta cooking water to the clam pan. Transfer the pasta to the pan, and cook, stirring, for an additional 2 minutes, until the pasta is tender but still firm to the bite.

6. Season with salt and pepper. Stir in the parsley and serve immediately.

bianco

Melanzane alla Parmigiana
Christmas Morning Baked Eggplant

SERVES 6–8

olive oil, for greasing
and brushing
3 eggplants, thinly sliced
10 ounces mozzarella cheese,
sliced
1 cup grated Parmesan
cheese
¼ cup fine dry bread crumbs
1 tablespoon butter, melted

TOMATO & BASIL SAUCE
2 tablespoons olive oil
4 shallots, finely chopped
2 garlic cloves, minced
1 (14½-ounce) can plum tomatoes
1 teaspoon sugar
8 fresh basil leaves, shredded
salt and pepper, to taste

1. Preheat the oven to 400°F. Grease a baking dish and two large baking sheets.

2. Arrange the eggplant slices in a single layer on the prepared baking sheets. Brush with oil and bake in the preheated oven for 15—20 minutes, until tender. Keep the oven on.

3. Meanwhile, make the sauce. Heat the oil in a saucepan, add the shallots, and cook for 5 minutes, until softened. Add the garlic and cook for a minute.

4. Add the tomatoes and break them up with a wooden spoon. Stir in the sugar and season with salt and pepper. Bring to a boil, reduce the heat, and simmer for about 10 minutes, until thickened. Stir in the basil.

5. Arrange half of the eggplant slices in the bottom of the prepared dish. Cover with half of the mozzarella, spoon half of the sauce over the top, and sprinkle with half of the Parmesan. Mix the remaining Parmesan with the bread crumbs. Repeat the layers, ending with the Parmesan mixture. Dot the top with the butter and bake for 25 minutes, until the topping is golden brown. Let stand for 5 minutes before serving.

Cime di Rapa Strascinate
Christmas Broccoli Rabe

1. Bring a large saucepan of lightly salted water to a boil. Meanwhile, remove and discard the thick ends of the broccoli rabe stems and any yellow leaves. Separate the thin stems with leaves from the thick stems with flower heads. Rinse well in several changes of cold water.

2. Add the thick stems to a boiling water and boil for 2 minutes, then add the thin stems and boil for 6—8 minutes, until all the stems are tender. Drain well, then set aside.

3. Heat the oil in a large skillet over medium—high heat. Add the chopped anchovies, garlic, shallots, and crushed red pepper and sauté, stirring to break down the anchovies, for 2—4 minutes, until the shallots are soft. Make sure that the garlic does not brown.

4. Stir the broccoli rabe into the anchovy mixture and season. Stir for 2—3 minutes, until the rabe is reheated and coated in the oil. Transfer the broccoli rabe to a serving platter and spoon any oil left in the pan over it. Slice each of the extra anchovy fillets lengthwise and arrange on top to garnish.

SERVES 4—6

2 bunches of broccoli rabe (rapini; about 2 pounds)
2 tablespoons olive oil
8 canned anchovy fillets in olive oil, drained and chopped, plus 2 extra fillets to garnish
4 large garlic cloves, thinly sliced
2 shallots, finely chopped
½ teaspoon crushed red pepper, or to taste
salt and pepper, to taste

Torta di Cioccolata & Pere

Genoese Chocolate & Pear Cake

1. Preheat the oven to 350°F. Grease an 8-inch springform round cake pan and line with parchment paper.

2. Melt the butter in a small saucepan, then set aside. Peel and quarter the pears, then remove and discard the cores. Brush the pears with lemon juice and set aside.

3. Put the eggs and sugar into a bowl and beat with an electric handheld mixer for 4—5 minutes, until light and fluffy but thick enough to leave a trail when the beaters are lifted. Beat in the vanilla extract.

4. Sift in the flour, cocoa powder, and baking powder. Lightly and quickly fold in the flour mixture, using a large metal spoon. Slowly drizzle the melted butter around the edge of the bowl and gently fold it in, then fold in the hazelnuts.

5 tablespoons butter, plus
    extra for greasing
2 Bosc pears
1 tablespoon lemon juice
2 extra-large eggs
1 cup granulated sugar
½ teaspoon vanilla extract
¾ cup Italian OO flour
    or all-purpose flour
¼ cup unsweetened cocoa powder
¾ teaspoon baking powder
½ cup blanched hazelnuts,
    chopped and toasted
confectioners' sugar, to
    decorate
mascarpone cheese, crème
    fraîche, or whipped crème,
    to serve

5. Pour the batter into the prepared pan. Arrange the pears, cored side down, in a spoked wheel pattern.

6. Bake in the preheated oven for 35—40 minutes, until firm to the touch and a toothpick inserted in the center comes out clean. Let cool in the pan for 5 minutes on a wire rack. Remove the side of the pan and then return the cake to the rack to cool completely.

7. Just before serving, generously dust the top of the cake with confectioners' sugar. Slice and serve with mascarpone cheese.

Panettone
Christmas Loaf

SERVES 8

10 cardamom pods
1 tablespoon butter, plus extra
   for greasing
2¼ cups white bread flour, plus
   extra for dusting
2 tablespoons sugar
½ teaspoon active dry yeast
1 teaspoon salt
grated rind of 1 lemon
1 teaspoon vanilla extract
⅔ cup milk
2 egg yolks
¼ cup chopped candied peel
⅔ cup golden raisins

1. Grease a 7-inch round cake pan. Crush the cardamom pods lightly in a mortar and pestle and discard the shells. Grind the cardamom seeds to a powder.

2. Rub the butter into the flour in a large bowl and add the sugar, yeast, salt, and cardamom powder. Stir to mix. Add the lemon rind, vanilla extract, milk, and egg yolks, and mix with a wooden spoon to make a soft dough.

3. Turn out the dough onto a floured work surface and knead for 10 minutes. Return the dough to the bowl, cover with plastic wrap, and let rise in a warm place for 2 hours or until doubled in size.

4. Return the dough to the lightly floured work surface and knock out the air in the dough with the palm of your hand. Knead in the candied peel and raisins until evenly distributed. Transfer to the prepared pan and cover with plastic wrap. Let rise again for another 2 hours or until doubled in size.

5. Preheat the oven to 300°F. Remove the plastic wrap from the prepared pan and bake in the preheated oven for 1 hour, until dark golden brown. Let cool in the pan for 20 minutes before running a spatula around the pan to loosen. Transfer the cake to a wire rack to cool completely.

1. Preheat the oven to 350°F. Line an 8-inch springform round cake pan with parchment paper.

2. Spread out the hazelnuts on a baking sheet and toast in the preheated oven for 10 minutes, until golden brown. Transfer the nuts to a dish towel and rub off the skins.

3. Meanwhile, spread out the almonds on a baking sheet and toast in the oven for 10 minutes, until golden. Watch carefully because they burn easily.

4. Reduce the oven temperature to 300°F. Chop all the nuts and place in a large bowl. Add the candied peel, apricots, pineapple, and orange rind to the nuts and mix well.

5. Sift the flour, cocoa, cinnamon, coriander, nutmeg, and cloves into the bowl and mix well.

6. Put the granulated sugar and honey into a saucepan and set over low heat, stirring, until the sugar has dissolved. Bring to a boil and cook for 5 minutes, until thickened and beginning to darken. Stir the nut mixture into the saucepan and remove from the heat.

7. Spoon the batter into the prepared cake pan and smooth the surface. Bake in the oven for 1 hour, then transfer to a wire rack to cool. When cold, carefully remove from the pan and peel off the parchment paper.

8. To serve, dust the top of the cake with confectioners' sugar and cut into thin wedges.

SERVES 14

1 cup hazelnuts
¾ cup almonds
½ cup chopped candied peel
½ cup finely chopped dried
  apricots
⅓ cup finely chopped candied
  pineapple
grated rind of 1 orange
½ cup all-purpose flour
2 tablespoons unsweetened
  cocoa powder
1 teaspoon ground cinnamon
¼ teaspoon ground coriander
¼ teaspoon freshly grated nutmeg
¼ teaspoon ground cloves
½ cup granulated sugar
¾ cup honey
confectioners' sugar,
  for dusting

Mama's Note:
Panforte is a traditional Christmas
dessert from Siena in Tuscany, dating
back to the thirteenth century.

Struffoli
- - - - - - -
Christmas
Honey Pastries

1. Sift together the flour and salt into a large bowl and make a well in the center. Add the eggs, butter, limoncello, and lemon rind to the well, then use your hands to combine all the ingredients to form a soft, sticky dough.

2. Turn out the dough onto a lightly floured surface and knead for about 5 minutes, until firm and smooth. Shape into a ball, wrap in plastic wrap, and set aside for at least 30 minutes.

3. Divide the dough into eight equal pieces. Work with one piece at a time and keep the remainder covered. On a lightly dusted work surface, roll one piece of dough into a thin rope, about 2 feet long and slightly more than ¼ inch thick. Cut it into ⅜-inch pieces then roll each piece into a ball slightly larger than a hazelnut. Set the balls aside and repeat with the remaining dough.

4. Heat enough oil for deep-frying in a heavy saucepan over high heat until it reaches 350—375°F, or until a cube of bread browns in 30 seconds. Add as many dough balls to the pan as will fit without overcrowding and fry for 2½—3½ minutes, until golden but not brown. Use a slotted spoon to transfer the fried balls to a plate lined with paper towels. Reheat the oil, if necessary, and repeat until all the dough balls have been fried.

5. Melt the honey in a large saucepan. Add the fried balls and stir. Stir in the peel, half the sprinkles, and the candied balls, then place on a plate. Sprinkle with the remaining sprinkles and serve.

SERVES 4

2⅓ cups Italian 00 flour
    or all-purpose flour,
    plus extra for dusting
pinch of salt
3 eggs, beaten
3 tablespoons butter, diced,
    at room temperature
1½ tablespoons limoncello, dry
    white wine, or orange juice
finely grated rind of 2 lemons
olive oil or sunflower oil,
    for deep-frying
¾ cup honey
¼ cup finely chopped candied
    peel
2 tablespoons sprinkles
1 tablespoon gold or silver
    candied balls

Ricciarelli
Almond Christmas Cookies

1. Preheat the oven to 300°F. Line a baking sheet with parchment paper. Put half of the confectioners' sugar into a shallow bowl and set aside.

2. Put the remaining confectioners' sugar, ground almonds, chopped almonds, and granulated sugar into a large bowl and stir together. Sift in the flour and baking powder and stir to combine.

3. In a separate bowl, beat the egg whites until they hold stiff peaks. Add the almond extract, sprinkle in the cream of tartar, and beat again. Beat 2 tablespoons of the egg whites into the almond mixture to loosen, then fold in the remaining egg whites.

4. Use a tablespoon to scoop up a small amount of the dough, then use another spoon to shape the dough into a flat oval or crescentlike shape. Gently drop into the bowl of confectioners' sugar and roll around until

MAKES 22–24

1⅔ cups confectioners' sugar
2 cups ground almonds
  (almond meal)
⅓ cup blanched almonds,
  chopped
¼ cup granulated sugar
½ cup Italian 00 flour
  or all-purpose flour
1 teaspoon baking powder
5 egg whites
¼ teaspoon almond extract
¼ teaspoon cream of tartar

it is coated. (Alternatively, shape the dough into walnut-size balls and drop them into the confectioners' sugar.)

5. Gently shake the cookie in your hand to reinforce the shape and remove the excess confectioners' sugar. Transfer to the prepared baking sheet and repeat with the remaining dough until it has all been used. Reserve any leftover confectioners' sugar.

6. Bake in the preheated oven for 15–20 minutes, until set and golden brown. Let cool on the baking sheet for 2 minutes, then transfer to a wire rack to cool completely, dusting with any leftover confectioners' sugar. Serve immediately or store in an airtight container for up to five days.

Celebrate the holidays—Italian style!

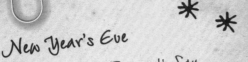

In Italy, we take our holidays seriously. And in Apulia, we are even more serious about making sure our holidays are not only filled with laughter and good times, but also the *cibo migliore*, the very best food!

New Year's Eve

Known as La Festa di San Silvestro, New Year's Eve is a time when the whole family gets together for a huge feast. What do you mean, so soon after Christmas? It's a whole week after! We always eat a meal made with lentils — they symbolize money and good fortune for the coming year. And afterward — fireworks, music, and dancing!

Easter

Next to Christmas, Easter is a time of great celebration in Italy. We have a phrase here, "Natale con i tuoi, Pasqua con chi vuoi" — Christmas with your family, Easter with your friends. What does that mean for Mama? It means Easter with family and friends! Beautiful Easter Lamb and my famous Florentine Easter Cake are always popular.

Carnevale

How do Italians prepare for Lent? By holding a season of parties and indulgences, of course! Carnevale starts on the Feast of the Epiphany, January 6, and lasts until Lent. Across all Italy there are parties, parades, and magnificent feasts. In Apulia, we are especially famous for our Cenci fritters at this time of year.

Valentine's Day

This beautiful celebration of amore began in ancient Rome—but in modern Italy the romance of the day is now almost second to a new tradition: that of cooking for each other. We do not do cards or flowers but something far more special. It is the only day of the year in which Alberto is allowed to prepare dinner for Mama!

Lenticchie San Silvestro

New Year's Eve Lentils

1. Place the lentils in a saucepan and cover with boiling water. Bring to a boil and boil for 10 minutes. Drain and set aside.

2. Heat the oil in a large skillet over medium heat and sauté the celery and leeks for 2—3 minutes, until softened but not browned. Stir in the garlic, sun-dried tomatoes, sage, and rosemary.

3. Add the cooked lentils, stock, and salt and pepper, then bring to a boil. Reduce the heat, cover, and simmer gently for 25—30 minutes or until the lentils are tender.

4. Stir in the artichokes and heat gently for 2—3 minutes. Serve immediately.

SERVES 4

1 cup green lentils
2 tablespoons olive oil
2 celery stalks, chopped
2 leeks, sliced
1 garlic clove, crushed
1 cup chopped sun-dried tomatoes
2 tablespoons chopped fresh sage
1 tablespoon chopped fresh rosemary
2 cups ham or vegetable stock
12 artichoke hearts from a jar
   or can, drained
salt and pepper, to taste

Agnello di Pasqua
Easter Roasted Lamb

SERVES 6

4 pound leg of lamb
2 garlic cloves, thinly sliced
2 tablespoons rosemary leaves
½ cup olive oil
18-24 new potatoes (about
   2 pounds), cut into
   1-inch cubes
6 fresh sage leaves, chopped
⅔ cup Marsala
salt and pepper, to taste

1. Preheat the oven to 425°F. Use a small knife to make incisions all over the lamb, then insert the garlic and about half of the rosemary leaves.

2. Place the lamb in a roasting pan and spoon half of the oil over it. Roast in the preheated oven for 15 minutes.

3. Reduce the oven temperature to 350°F. Remove the lamb from the oven and season with salt and pepper. Turn the lamb over, return to the oven, and roast for an additional hour.

4. Put the potatoes in a separate roasting pan, add the remaining oil, and toss to coat. Sprinkle with the remaining rosemary and the sage. Place the potatoes in the oven with the lamb and roast for 40 minutes.

5. Remove the lamb from the oven, turn it over, and pour the Marsala over the lamb. Return to the oven and cook for an additional 15 minutes, or until cooked to taste.

6. Transfer the lamb to a carving board and cover with aluminum foil. Remove the potatoes from the oven and set aside. Place the juices from the meat in a saucepan over high heat and bring to a boil. Continue to boil until thickened and syrupy. Carve the lamb into slices and serve with the potatoes and meat juices.

Schiacciata

Florentine Easter Cake

1. Grease a 10 x 6-inch baking pan or roasting pan with lard. Stir together the flour, granulated sugar, yeast, salt, and orange rind in a large bowl. Add the lard and work in until the mixture resembles coarse crumbs. Make a well in the center, add the orange juice, egg yolks, and water, and beat together until a soft, sticky dough forms. Slowly add extra water if the dough is too stiff.

2. Turn out the dough onto a floured work surface and knead for 10 minutes, until the lard has melted and is distributed and the dough is smooth. Wash and dry the mixing bowl, then grease with lard.

3. Shape the dough into a ball, roll around in the bowl, and cover with plastic wrap. Set aside in a warm place until doubled in volume, which can take up to 2 hours.

3 cups Italian 00 flour
   or white bread flour, plus
   extra for dusting
¼ cup granulated sugar
2¼ teaspoons active dry yeast
pinch of salt
finely grated rind of
   2 large oranges
4 tablespoons lard or butter,
   diced, plus extra for
   greasing
3 tablespoons freshly squeezed
   orange juice
2 egg yolks, beaten
¾–1 cup water, heated to 115°F
confectioners' sugar, to
   decorate (optional)

4. Turn out the dough and lightly knead. Press it into the prepared pan. Cover with a sheet of greased plastic wrap and flatten and level the dough to not more than ½ inch thick. Let rise for 20 minutes.

5. Meanwhile, preheat the oven to 375°F. Remove the plastic wrap and bake the cake in the preheated oven for 30—35 minutes, or until it is golden, about 1 inch high, and coming away from the side of the pan. Transfer the pan to a wire rack and thickly dust the top of the cake with confectioners' sugar, if desired. Let the cake rest in the pan on the rack to cool completely.

6. Cut into 12 squares and serve.

Chiacchiere
Carnival Ricotta Fritters

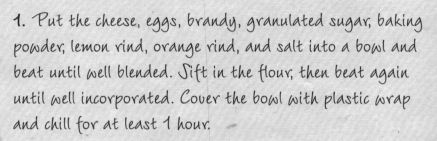

MAKES 24

1¼ cups ricotta cheese
2 eggs, beaten
3 tablespoons brandy or rum
1½ tablespoons granulated sugar
2 tablespoons baking powder
1 teaspoon finely grated
   lemon rind
1 teaspoon finely grated
   orange rind
pinch of salt
1⅓ cups all-purpose flour
sunflower oil, for deep-frying,
   plus extra for greasing
confectioners' sugar, to decorate

1. Put the cheese, eggs, brandy, granulated sugar, baking powder, lemon rind, orange rind, and salt into a bowl and beat until well blended. Sift in the flour, then beat again until well incorporated. Cover the bowl with plastic wrap and chill for at least 1 hour.

2. When ready to fry, heat enough oil for deep-frying in a heavy saucepan over high heat until it reaches 350—375°F, or until a cube of bread browns in 30 seconds. Preheat the oven to 300°F. Line a heatproof plate with paper towels and set aside.

3. Grease a large spoon with oil, then use it to drop as many spoonfuls of the batter into the hot oil that will fit in the pan without overcrowding. Fry for 3—5 minutes, gently turning the fritters over once, until they rise to the surface, puff, and turn brown.

4. Use a slotted spoon to remove the fritters from the oil and drain well on paper towels. Transfer to the lined plate and keep warm in the oven while you fry the remaining mixture. Reheat the oil between batches and regrease the spoon, if necessary. When all the batter has been fried, dust the fritters with confectioners' sugar and serve immediately.

Cenci
Carnival Peel Fritters

1. Place the golden raisins, candied peel, grappa, and lemon rind in a bowl and let soak for 1 hour. Place the flour, sugar, and yeast in a bowl and stir in the egg with enough of the milk to make a thick batter. Stir the golden raisin mixture and the pine nuts into the bowl. Cover and let rest in a warm place for about 3 hours, or until spongy and doubled in size.

2. When ready to fry, heat enough oil for deep-frying in a heavy saucepan over high heat until it reaches 350—375°F, or until a cube of bread browns in 30 seconds. Preheat the oven to 300°F. Line a heatproof plate with paper towels and set aside.

3. Grease a large spoon with oil, then use it to drop as many spoonfuls of the batter into the hot oil that will fit in the pan. Fry for 3—5 minutes, turning the fritters over once, until they rise to the surface and turn brown. Use a slotted spoon to remove the fritters and transfer to the lined plate. Keep them warm in the oven while you fry the remaining batter. Reheat the oil between batches and regrease the spoon, if necessary. Dust with confectioners' sugar and serve immediately.

MAKES 24

⅔ cup golden raisins
⅓ cup chopped candied peel
3 tablespoons grappa or rum
finely grated rind of 1 lemon
3¼ cups all-purpose flour
¼ cup granulated sugar
2¼ teaspoons active dry yeast
1 medium egg, beaten
about 1 cup lukewarm milk
⅓ cup pine nuts
sunflower oil, for deep-frying, plus extra for greasing
confectioners' sugar, for dusting

Delizioso Desserts & Gelati

Mama once heard a fool declare "Always leave an audience wanting more." What? These are the words of a miser! Mama never leaves anyone wanting more! It is always a source of constant pride to me that nobody has ever left my table unsatisfied—and, once you learn the secrets of Mama's *delizioso* desserts and gelati, it should be the same for you! Too many cooks think of the dessert as an afterthought to the meal, something that can be squeezed in if there's room. Not so in Italy! Here, we think of a dessert as a miniature work of art in itself, as worthy of as much attention and time as anything else you might put on your table. Just think of Biscotti, Zabaglione, Cannoli, Tiramisu . . . or Chocolate Cake, Gelati, Panna Cotta. Never let it be said anyone has ever left my table wanting more!

Gelato di Lampone
Raspberry Gelato

1. Check through the raspberries for any imperfections and discard any that are past their best. Hull the remaining raspberries and place in a bowl.

2. Puree the raspberries in a blender or food processor, strain through a fine-meshed, nonmetallic strainer to remove all the seeds, then set aside.

3. Put the milk and sugar into a saucepan and place over medium heat, stirring thoroughly until the sugar dissolves. Put the cornstarch into a small bowl and stir in ¼ cup of the warm milk, stirring until smooth.

4. Stir the cornstarch mixture into the milk pan, increase the heat, and stir continuously for 6—8 minutes, until just below boiling point, or until the mixture thickens. If there are any lumps, push through a strainer.

MAKES ABOUT 3½ CUPS

3 cups fresh raspberries
1½ cups milk
¼ cup superfine sugar or
   granulated sugar
1½ tablespoons cornstarch

5. Pour the mixture into a bowl, stir in the raspberry puree, and let cool. Transfer to a freezerproof bowl and freeze. It does not need any beating while it freezes.

6. Transfer to the refrigerator 30 minutes before serving to soften. Serve in small bowls before the gelato gets too soft.

Mama's Tip:
For all my hints and tips on making the perfect gelati, go to pages 194 and 195.

Tartufo

Chocolate Ice Cream Balls

1. Place four ¾-cup freezer-proof bowls in the freezer.

2. Transfer the ice cream to a large bowl and let rest until just beginning to soften, then stir in the chocolate chips. Remove the bowls from the freezer and divide the ice cream mixture among them. Push a cherry into the center of each and smooth over the hole. Place in the freezer for at least 2 hours, or until firm.

3. Bring a small saucepan of water to simmering point. Working with one bowl at a time, submerge each bowl in the water for 5—10 seconds, until the ice cream looks like it is softening around the edge. Invert the bowl onto a plate, give a good firm shake, and the ice cream should drop out. If it doesn't, return the bowl to the water for an additional 5 seconds and try again.

4. Sprinkle one-quarter of the chocolate sprinkles over the ice cream ball, using a small knife to make sure the surface is coated. Repeat with the remaining balls.

5. If not serving immediately, place the bowl over the coated ice cream ball and invert the plate. Cover the top with freezer-proof plastic wrap and return the ball to the freezer until required.

6. When ready to serve, transfer each ball to a serving bowl and let soften for 5—10 minutes. If you want an extra chocolate hit, spoon some chocolate sauce over the top just before serving.

MAKES 4

3 cups chocolate ice cream
½ cup semisweet chocolate chips,
   or 4 ounces semisweet
   chocolate, chopped
4 candied cherries
½ cup chocolate vermicelli
1 quantity Chocolate Sauce,
   see page 198, to serve
   (optional)

Mama's Tip:
Don't let the ice cream soften too much in step 2 before you add the chocolate chips, or they will all sink to the bottom of the bowl.

Making gorgeous gelati

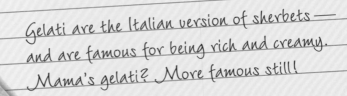

Gelati are the Italian version of sherbets — and are famous for being rich and creamy. Mama's gelati? More famous still!

In the north, gelati are made with an egg custard and include cream, similar to ice cream. In Apulia, however, the gelati do not contain cream or eggs.

The basic ingredients for traditional gelati are whole milk, sugar, cornstarch, and your choice of flavoring. Because this style of gelati has a lower butterfat content than ice cream made with cream, any flavorings you do add — especially *frutta fresca* or fresh fruit purees — really stand out.

Making an authentic gelato is quick and easy. Even without an ice cream maker, you will get a rich and creamy result — and you don't have to beat the mixture as it freezes!

Two tips from Mama will guarantee success. Do not let the milk boil at any point, because too hot a temperature will destroy the thickening qualities of the cornstarch. And always stir a few tablespoonfuls of the hot milk into the cornstarch before adding it to the saucepan. This prevents lumps from forming. If lumps do form, however, use a wire whisk to beat the mixture while it heats. If the lumps don't dissolve, strain the mixture through a strainer before you add any flavoring.

Then all you have to do is let the gelato mixture cool completely and stir well before putting it in the freezer.

Mama's traditional gelato has a shorter freezer life than custard-base ice creams. The texture is best if it is eaten within three days of freezing. Transfer the gelato to the refrigerator to soften about 20 minutes before serving. In Italy, we like our gelati slightly softer than other ice creams.

Sorbetto di Prosecco alle Uve
Prosecco Sorbet with Grapes

SERVES 4

¾ cup granulated sugar
⅔ cup water
thinly pared strip of lemon zest
juice of 1 lemon
1½ cups Prosecco
grapes, halved, and fresh mint
   sprigs, to decorate

1. Place the sugar and water in a saucepan with the lemon zest.

2. Stir over low heat until the sugar dissolves, then boil for 2—3 minutes to reduce by half.

3. Let cool and remove the lemon zest.

4. Combine the sugar syrup with the lemon juice and Prosecco, then churn the mixture in an ice cream maker, following the manufacturers' directions.

5. Alternatively, pour into a freezer-proof container and freeze, uncovered, beating at hourly intervals until frozen.

6. When ready to serve, let rest at room temperature to soften slightly, then scoop the sorbet into sundae glasses.

7. Decorate with grape halves and mint sprigs before serving.

Cassata
Sicilian Ice Cream

1. Press the ricotta through a strainer into a bowl, using a wooden spoon.

2. Stir in the confectioners' sugar and orange flower water, beating until smooth.

3. Whip the cream until thick enough to hold its shape, then fold into the ricotta mixture.

4. Churn the mixture in an ice cream maker following the manufacturers' directions. Alternatively, pour into a freezer-proof container and freeze, uncovered, until slushy.

5. Fold in the candied peel, candied angelica, candied cherries, chocolate, and pistachio nuts.

6. Transfer the mixture to a 1¼-quart deep, round freezer-proof bowl and freeze until firm. Let rest at room temperature for 10—15 minutes before turning out.

7. Cut the ice cream into wedges and serve on a plate with candied fruit.

SERVES 6–8

1¾ cups ricotta cheese
1½ cups confectioners' sugar
1 teaspoon orange flower water
1 cup heavy cream
½ cup chopped candied peel
¼ cup chopped candied angelica or extra candied peel
¼ cup chopped candied cherries
2 ounces semisweet chocolate, chopped
⅓ cup chopped pistachio nuts
candied fruit, to serve

Gelato di Pistacchi
Pistachio Gelato

1. Preheat the oven to 350°F. Bring a saucepan of water to a boil. Add the nuts and boil for 30 seconds. Drain and shake well, then peel off the skins. Place the nuts on a baking sheet and toast in the preheated oven for 5 minutes. Transfer the nuts to a blender or food processor.

2. Pour the milk into a saucepan and heat over high heat until just below boiling point. Pour about one-third of the milk over the nuts and blend the mixture until a thick paste forms. Stir the paste into the pan with the milk, cover, and set aside for 4 hours to infuse. Strain, pressing down firmly, then discard the nuts and reserve the liquid.

3. Reheat the pistachio-flavored liquid over low heat. Add the sugar and stir until it dissolves. Put the cornstarch into a bowl and whisk in ¼ cup of the liquid, whisking until smooth. Stir the cornstarch mixture into the pan, increase the heat, and stir continuously until just below boiling point, then continue to stir for 8—10 minutes, until the mixture thickens. If there are any lumps, push the mixture through a strainer.

4. Pour the mixture into a bowl and let cool. Transfer to a freezer-proof serving bowl and freeze. Transfer to the refrigerator 30 minutes before serving to soften. Serve scoops in individual bowls.

5. Meanwhile, to make the sauce, gently melt the chocolate in a heatproof bowl set over a saucepan of gently simmering water, stirring until smooth. Stir in the cream, vanilla, and butter, stirring until smooth and shiny. Remove from the heat and let cool, then spoon over the gelato.

MAKES ABOUT 3½ CUPS

1½ cups shelled, unsalted
  pistachio nuts
3 cups milk
½ cup superfine or granulated
  sugar
3 tablespoons cornstarch

CHOCOLATE SAUCE
6 ounces semisweet chocolate,
  finely chopped
¼ cup heavy cream
¼ teaspoon vanilla extract
1 tablespoon salted butter

Mama's Tip:
Peeling the nuts is not totally
necessary, but it does give the
finished dish a clear, fresh
color. You can skip the step
but the appearance will be
less appealing.

Granita di Limone
Lemon Granita

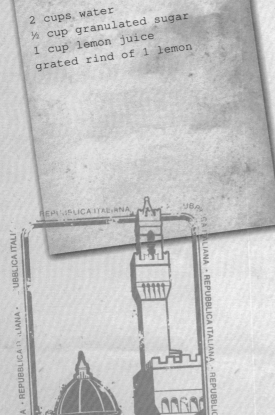

SERVES 4

2 cups water
½ cup granulated sugar
1 cup lemon juice
grated rind of 1 lemon

1. Heat the water in a heavy saucepan over low heat. Add the sugar and stir until it has dissolved. Bring to a boil, then remove from the heat and let cool.

2. Stir the lemon juice and rind into the cooled syrup.

3. Pour the mixture into a freezer-proof container and freeze for 3–4 hours.

4. Remove the container from the freezer and dip the bottom into hot water. Turn out the block of ice and chop coarsely, then place in a heavy-duty food processor and process until it forms small crystals.

5. Spoon into sundae glasses and serve immediately.

Cannoli Siciliani
Chocolate Orange Cannoli

1. Beat the egg and Marsala together. Put the flour, sugar, and salt into a food processor and blend. With the motor running, slowly pour in the egg mixture until the ingredients just come together to form a dough. Turn out the dough onto a lightly floured work surface and knead. Roll into a ball, wrap in plastic wrap, and chill for at least 1 hour.

2. Meanwhile, to make the filling, beat together the cheese, brandy, and vanilla extract until creamy. Sift in the cocoa powder and confectioners' sugar and stir in the candied oranges, chocolate, orange rind, and cinnamon. Cover and chill until required. Cut the dough into four equal pieces. Use a pasta machine to roll one piece into a strip about 1¾ feet long, or roll out on a lightly floured work surface until the dough is thin enough to see through. Cut out 1½ –inch squares. Brush some cannoli tubes with oil and diagonally roll a piece of dough around each. Use a dab of water to seal the corners where they meet and press firmly.

3. Heat enough oil for deep-frying until it reaches 350—375°F, or until a cube of bread browns in 30 seconds. Add 2 or 3 cannoli tubes at a time and fry until the pastry turns golden brown and crisp. Using a slotted spoon, remove the tubes and drain on paper towels. Continue until all the dough is used, gently sliding the shells off the tubes and regreasing before using again. Store in an airtight container for up to three days until required. Just before serving, use a pastry bag or a spoon to fill the tubes from both ends. If you fill the cannoli in advance, they will become soggy. Sift over some confectioners' sugar and serve immediately.

MAKES 20–24

1 egg
2 tablespoons Marsala
1⅓ cups Italian 00 flour or
   all-purpose flour, plus extra
   for dusting
2 teaspoons granulated sugar
pinch of salt
sunflower oil, for greasing
   and deep-frying
confectioners' sugar, to decorate

CHOCOLATE & ORANGE FILLING
3 cups ricotta cheese
2 tablespoons brandy
2 teaspoons vanilla extract
2 tablespoons unsweetened
   cocoa powder
¼ cup confectioners' sugar,
   plus extra to decorate
¼ cup chopped candied oranges
¼ cup chopped semisweet chocolate
finely grated rind of 2 oranges
pinch of ground cinnamon

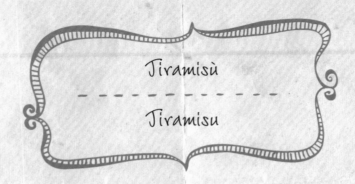

Tiramisù
- - - - - - - - - - - -
Tiramisu

1. Beat the egg yolks with the sugar and vanilla extract in a heatproof bowl set over a saucepan of barely simmering water.

2. When the mixture is pale and the beaters leave a ribbon trail when lifted, remove the bowl from the heat and set aside to cool. Beat occasionally to prevent a skin from forming.

3. When the egg yolk mixture is cool, beat in the mascarpone until thoroughly combined.

4. Beat the egg whites in a separate, spotlessly clean bowl until they form soft peaks, then gently fold them into the mascarpone mixture.

5. Combine the coffee and rum in a shallow dish. Briefly dip eight of the ladyfingers in the mixture, then arrange in the bottom of a deep, wide serving dish.

6. Spoon one-third of the mascarpone mixture on top, spreading it out evenly. Repeat the layers twice, finishing with the mascarpone mixture. Chill for at least 1 hour.

7. Sift the cocoa evenly over the top and sprinkle with the chocolate. Serve immediately.

SERVES 6

4 egg yolks
½ cup granulated sugar
1 teaspoon vanilla extract
2 cups mascarpone cheese
2 egg whites
¾ cup strong black coffee
½ cup rum or brandy
24 ladyfingers
2 tablespoons unsweetened
cocoa powder
2 tablespoons finely grated
semisweet chocolate

Torta di Ricotta al Forno

Italian–Style Cheesecake

Mama's Tip:
Soak some golden raisins in the Marsala for 30 minutes, then add to the cake batter with the almonds.

SERVES 4–6

butter, for greasing
1½ cups ricotta cheese
3 egg yolks, beaten
½ cup superfine or granulated sugar
¼ cup Marsala or rum
½ cup ground almonds (almond meal)
finely grated rind of
  1 lemon or 1 small orange
confectioners' sugar, to decorate

1. Preheat the oven to 350°F. Grease a 7-inch springform round cake pan and set aside.

2. Use a large metal spoon to push the cheese through a strainer into a bowl. Add the egg yolks and superfine sugar and beat until blended and the sugar dissolves. Stir in the Marsala, ground almonds, and lemon rind.

3. Pour the batter into the prepared pan and smooth the surface. Bake in the preheated oven for 1—1¼ hours, or until the cheesecake is set and coming away from the side of the pan.

4. Turn off the oven and let the cheesecake rest inside the oven for 2—3 hours with the door propped open.

5. When the cheesecake is cool, carefully remove it from the pan and transfer to a serving plate. Dust with confectioners' sugar just before serving.

Panna Cotta con Prugne
Panna Cotta with Spiced Plums

SERVES 4

4 sheets gelatin
1¼ cups milk
1 cup mascarpone cheese
½ cup sugar
1 vanilla bean, halved lengthwise

SPICED PLUMS
8 red plums, halved and stoned
3 tablespoons honey
1 cinnamon stick
thinly pared strip of orange zest
1 tablespoon balsamic vinegar

1. Soak the gelatin sheets in ¼ cup of the milk for 10 minutes.

2. Place the remaining milk, the mascarpone, sugar, and vanilla bean in a saucepan and heat gently, stirring until smooth, then bring to a boil.

3. Remove from the heat, discard the vanilla bean, and add the gelatin mixture, stirring until completely dissolved.

4. Pour into four 1-cup individual dessert molds. Let chill in the refrigerator until set.

5. To make the spiced plums, place the plums, honey, cinnamon stick, orange zest, and vinegar in a saucepan. Cover and cook gently for 10 minutes, or until the plums are tender.

6. Dip the bottom of each mold quickly in hot water and turn out onto a serving plate.

7. Serve the panna cotta with the spiced plums on the side.

Torta Caprese
Chocolate & Almond Tart

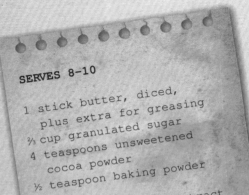

SERVES 8–10

1 stick butter, diced,
   plus extra for greasing
⅔ cup granulated sugar
4 teaspoons unsweetened
   cocoa powder
½ teaspoon baking powder
4 eggs
¼ teaspoon vanilla extract
2 tablespoons Strega,
   Marsala, or orange juice
4 ounces semisweet chocolate,
   finely chopped
2 cups ground almonds
   (almond meal)
confectioners' sugar and
   vanilla ice cream, to serve

1. Preheat the oven to 350°F. Grease an 8-inch springform round cake pan and line with parchment paper.

2. Put the butter and sugar into a large bowl and beat with an electric handheld mixer until smooth and creamy. Sift in the cocoa powder and baking powder and beat them in, then add the eggs, one at a time, beating until each is incorporated before adding the next. Beat in the vanilla extract and Strega.

3. Add the chocolate and ground almonds and stir. Pour the batter into the prepared pan and level the surface.

4. Bake in the preheated oven for 1—1¼ hours, or until firm to the touch and a toothpick inserted into the center comes out clean.

5. Let cool for 5 minutes in the pan, then remove from the tin and transfer to a wire rack to cool completely.

6. Just before serving, generously dust the top with confectioners' sugar. Serve with a scoop of vanilla ice cream.

Torta di Cioccolato
Rich Italian Chocolate Cake

SERVES 6-8

butter, for greasing
flour, for dusting
1⅓ cups hazelnuts
8 ounces bittersweet chocolate
1½ cups blanched almonds
⅓ cup brandy
2 tablespoons espresso coffee
1 teaspoon ground cinnamon
2 tablespoons milk
1 cup superfine sugar
   or granulated sugar
5 extra-large eggs, separated,
   at room temperature
mascarpone cheese, to serve

1. Preheat the oven to 350°F. Grease a 10-inch springform round cake pan with butter and sprinkle with flour.

2. Place the hazelnuts on a baking sheet and bake in the preheated oven for 5 minutes, then let cool. While the nuts are baking, chop the chocolate into small pieces and place in a food processor with the almonds. Process until the mixture resembles bread crumbs.

3. Transfer the mixture to a bowl and stir in the brandy, coffee, cinnamon, milk, and half the sugar. Add the egg yolks, one at a time, and continue to mix. Rub the hazelnuts to remove the skins.

4. Place the hazelnuts in the processor. Process until coarser than the almonds and chocolate. Add to the cake batter and combine well. In a clean bowl, beat the egg whites until stiff, add the remaining sugar, and continue to beat. Fold the egg whites into the cake batter with a large metal spoon, a few spoonfuls at a time, with a cutting movement of the spoon so that you don't knock out too much air in the egg whites. Gently spoon the batter into the prepared cake pan and bake in the center of the oven for 1 hour, until a toothpick inserted into the center comes out clean. Turn out onto a wire rack to cool. Serve with mascarpone cheese.

Pesche e Amaretti
Peaches with Amaretti

1. Preheat the oven to 350°F. Lightly grease a baking dish large enough to hold the peach halves in a single layer.

2. Use a small teaspoon to make holes in the center of each peach half, slightly deeper and wider than the hole made by the pit. Transfer the removed flesh to a bowl.

3. Add the amaretti, egg yolk, butter, and half of the sugar to the peach flesh and beat together. Divide this mixture evenly among the peach halves, spooning into a slight mound.

4. Place the filled peach halves in the prepared dish. Pour the wine over and around the halves. Sprinkle the filled peach halves with the remaining sugar.

SERVES 4

4 peaches, halved and pitted
1 cup crushed amaretti
1 egg yolk, beaten
2 tablespoons butter, softened,
  plus extra for greasing
2 tablespoons packed light
  brown sugar
⅔ cup dry white wine
mascarpone cheese, to serve

5. Bake in the preheated oven for 25—30 minutes, or until the peaches are tender and starting to brown. Serve immediately, or let cool before serving, with mascarpone cheese.

Mama's Tip:
Use Marsala instead of wine if you prefer a sweeter finish—peaches with Marsala is a traditional Italian flavor combination.

1. Preheat the oven to 350°F and line two baking sheets with parchment paper.

2. Coarsely chop the almonds, leaving some whole. Mix together the flour, sugar, baking powder, and cinnamon in a mixing bowl. Stir in all of the almonds.

3. Beat the eggs with the vanilla extract in a small bowl, then add to the flour mixture and mix together to form a firm dough. Turn out the dough onto a lightly floured surface and knead lightly.

4. Divide the dough in half and shape each piece into a log about 2 inches wide. Transfer to the prepared baking sheets and sprinkle with sugar. Bake in the preheated oven for 20–25 minutes or until firm.

5. Remove from the oven and let cool slightly, then transfer to a cutting board and cut into ½-inch slices. Meanwhile, reduce the oven temperature to 325°F.

6. Arrange the slices, cut side down, on the baking sheets. Bake in the preheated oven for 15–20 minutes, until dry and crisp. Transfer to a wire rack to cool.

7. Store in an airtight container for up to a week to keep crisp.

1¾ cups whole blanched
   almonds
1⅔ cups all-purpose flour,
   plus extra for dusting
¾ cup sugar, plus extra for
   sprinkling
1 teaspoon baking powder
½ teaspoon ground cinnamon
2 eggs
2 teaspoons vanilla extract

Zabaglione con Frutti d'Estate
Zabaglione with Summer Fruit

1. Put the fruit into a nonmetallic bowl and stir in the vanilla sugar and orange rind. Cover with plastic wrap and set aside for at least 1 hour.

2. Select a heatproof bowl that will fit in a saucepan over about 2 inches of boiling water without the bottom of the bowl touching the water and set aside.

3. Bring a saucepan of water to just below boiling point.

4. Put the egg yolks and sugar into the heatproof bowl and beat with an electric handheld mixer until blended and the sugar has dissolved. Stir in the Marsala.

5. Place the bowl over the simmering water and beat for 5—8 minutes, until the mixture is thick, creamy, and holds soft peaks. Make sure the bottom of the bowl does not touch the water, or the eggs will scramble.

6. Stir the fruit and adjust the vanilla sugar, if necessary. Divide the fruit among four glass bowls and spoon the hot zabaglione over.

7. Serve immediately with ladyfingers on the side.

SERVES 4

2 cups mixed berries, such as
  hulled, sliced strawberries,
  raspberries, blackberries,
  and blueberries
1 tablespoon vanilla-flavor
  sugar, or to taste
finely grated rind of 1 orange
3 egg yolks
¼ cup superfine sugar or
  granulated sugar
⅓ cup Marsala
ladyfingers, to serve

Fragole Balsamiche

Strawberries with Balsamic Vinegar

SERVES 4

1 pound strawberries, plus extra if needed

2 tablespoons sugar, or to taste

1 tablespoon good-quality balsamic vinegar, or to taste

pepper, to serve

1. Pick through the strawberries to make sure all are of the best quality and remove any particularly soft fruit. Hull and halve the strawberries, placing them in a small bowl as you work.

2. Place the sugar and vinegar into a nonmetallic bowl and gently mix together. Add the strawberries and stir to mix together thoroughly. Let rest at room temperature for at least 1 hour but not more than 3 hours.

3. When ready to serve, stir again and add extra sugar or vinegar, if desired.

4. Grind some pepper over the top of the strawberries and serve immediately.